LIVING THE DREAM

LESSONS FROM THE LIFE OF JOSEPH

DAVE SMITH

CWR

Acknowledgements

Special thanks to my wise and lovely wife Karen and to my beautiful daughters, Emily and Annabel for their comments: you're the best! Many thanks, too, to Tim Pettingale for his encouragement and advice in the completion of this project. Thanks also to the amazing team and church at KingsGate and to some wonderful friends and fellow leaders across the body of Christ. Eternal thanks to the Lord for His love, grace and fellowship.

Editing, design and production by CWR

Printed in the UK by Linney Group

ISBN 978-1-78259-665-3

Contents

Foreword

He was a somewhat unusual childhood hero, but then I was probably a somewhat unusual child (those who know me as an adult would suggest that it's likely). He was Popeye the Sailor Man. Clay pipe permanently clamped in his jaws, with an Adam's apple as big as a melon, Popeye had an unhealthy preoccupation with the stick-thin Olive Oyl (that lady needed to eat a cheeseburger!). Popeye was brash and bold. He had a rather strange laugh – a high-pitched giggle that seemed incongruous for a sailor – but he made up for it with his muscles of iron. I loved him and was even tempted to try eating the fuel that gave him his strength: spinach.

But Popeye had a major fault line. He had a saying that I felt uncomfortable with – one that seemed to signal a white flag of defeat:

'I yam what I yam
And that's all what I yam
I'm Popeye the Sailor Man.'

Perhaps he was just saying, 'This is me, get over it!' (a philosophy that, sadly, even a few Christians embrace). But I took it to mean that he had sentenced himself to sameness. Who he was and what he'd become was fixed. Fine, I suppose, if you like being a sailor man, but generally an unfortunate way to live – and hardly hopeful.

Popeye probably wouldn't read *Living the Dream*. It would shatter his hopeless illusions if he discovered that we can be different, achieve much, grow daily and flourish, even in hardship. But I'm glad that you're a reader, because although there's much to inspire in this book, inspiration isn't enough. The world is full of 'inspiring' hucksters who set out their gaudy stalls of empty promises and slick slogans. The last thing we need is another seminar on self-improvement or a vacuous motivational speech.

But Dave Smith is not one for empty waffle. If you're going to talk about living the dream, it's rather helpful if you've lived it yourself, to state the obvious. I have watched and marvelled over the last decade as Dave and his wife, Karen, have walked with God with a trust that is intimate, a faith that is very rare, and with leadership skills that have caused so many in the Peterborough area to want to walk with Jesus and become part of KingsGate. They have, and are, living the dream.

What is the dream? The widescreen version is what Tom Wright calls 'the big fat story of God'. It's the blockbuster epic of the dealings of God with planet Earth through people. It is the as yet unfinished story that we have been invited into – and that means that Joseph's story is our story, as are the stories of Esther, Moses, Peter and Ruth.

But there is a micro to the macro, as Dave reminds us. Far from being lumped into an epic community-sized project, God has dreams for each of us – an individual purpose we can fulfil. Dave reminds us that there are 'Monday morning' dreams for us to dream, as well as for Sundays. God is very much at work in His world, not just His Church. He is not a localised deity who lives in the church car park. This book helps inspire us to connect with those divine dreams.

Reading this, you'll be more than inspired – you will be nourished, because this is biblical material, expounded well. It's practical, accessible, honest stuff.

As you read, I pray that you'll find hope, grace and faith. And while spinach might be to your taste, forget the 'I yams' of Popeye. The 'I Ams' of God are a far better foundation.

Jeff Lucas

Introduction

The story of Joseph is a truly inspiring account of someone who literally 'lived his dream'. It starts with a picture of a spoilt 17-year-old from a dysfunctional family who received a dramatic dream of future greatness. Clearly unprepared to live the dream, he underwent a long, hard 13-year period of testing and preparation, before experiencing sudden and dramatic promotion to a position of huge influence and affluence at the age of 30. Remarkably, he managed to stay at the top for a full 80 years without compromising his integrity or jeopardising his key relationships, before finishing well and leaving a great legacy for the next generation. By any standards, it is an outstanding story of preparation, promotion and prominence, with more drama than a soap opera and with a truly happy ending!

The colourful events of Joseph's life can be found in Genesis 37–50, and can be interpreted on a number of levels. First, they are a historical account of Jacob's favourite son, who became a bridge between God's covenant promises to Abraham and his saving acts through Moses. Second, they tell the story of a Hebrew man, betrayed by his brothers, nearly killed and yet gloriously vindicated to bring salvation to Israel and the nations – thereby foreshadowing Jesus Christ. Third, as an inspiring account of God's sovereign work in a person's life, the Joseph story is of great encouragement to all believers in all times and places. Fourth, as a study of a great administrator, businessman and national ruler, it is of particular help to leaders both in the marketplace and in the Church. Fifth, it has prophetic application to God's people collectively – to a 'Joseph generation', called by God to bring salvation to a world suffering spiritual, moral and economic famine.

I first taught on the topic of 'Living the dream' to our own KingsGate congregation in Peterborough in the autumn of 2006. After several years of planning, praying, battling and building, we had finally moved into our wonderful new church building – and so this series was of timely encouragement. Since then I have taught on 'Lessons from the life of

Joseph' in many forums, from large celebration gatherings to smaller conferences for church leaders, to Bible studies for Christian MPs and workers in Parliament, and have observed many greatly helped, encouraged and challenged by this remarkable biblical biography.

For me, Joseph has been an inspiration. Saved at 19 while at university and called to start the church in Peterborough at 25, I know the power of receiving a 'dream' from the Lord, embracing His preparation, and experiencing His favour and blessing. You too may be a young person starting out on the journey of life. If so, Joseph has much to teach you. But if like me you are at mid-life or entering your later years then there is still much to learn! There are new dreams to dream, new tests to pass, new blessings to experience and, of course, the promise of finishing well and leaving a great legacy. Because the Joseph story is exactly this – a story of one person's life – I believe it has the power to speak to us through all the seasons of our life. Whatever age you are or whatever stage of life you are in, my prayer is that the Lord will use this book to help transform the rest of your life.

CHAPTER 1

DREAM THE DREAM

If we, like Joseph, are to live the dream we first need to dream the dream – that is, to discover God's sovereign and unique plan for each of our lives. I use the term 'dream' because that is how God spoke to and revealed His plan to Joseph, in a night dream. But God speaks to people in many different ways (as we shall see later), through words, pictures, promptings and 'visions' during the day. I will use the terms 'visions' and 'dreams' interchangeably to refer to God speaking to us of something He has planned that has yet to come to pass.

Having a vision or dream for the future is something that often comes naturally to young people who, like the 17-year-old Joseph, have seemingly all of life before them. But whether you are young, middle-aged or older, whether you know God or not, it is time to dream!

Why? Because...

God has a great dream for your life!

The sovereign creator God has a plan for your life that predated your birth. That's great news! In Joseph's case, we can see the plan of God prevailing in the very circumstances of his birth:

> 'God remembered Rachel; he listened to her and enabled her to conceive. She became pregnant and gave birth to a son ... She named him Joseph' (Gen. 30:22–24)

While your conception may not have been the direct result of God answering prayer, nevertheless God was involved in planning your life even before birth. Before you thought of God, He first thought of you. Even if your parents didn't plan for you and you have often felt that you are an 'accident', please realise that you are no accident! Like Joseph, God planned for you to be born into a particular family at a particular place and time in history, to fulfil His special purposes in and through you.

God's sovereignty over the whole human race is highlighted in a remarkable speech by the apostle Paul to the pagan philosophers in Athens:

'he himself gives everyone life and breath and everything else. From one man he made all the nations, that they should inhabit the whole earth; and he marked out their appointed times in history and the boundaries of their lands. God did this so that they would seek him and perhaps reach out for him and find him, though he is not far from any one of us.'
(Acts 17:25–27)

Whether you know Him yet or not, God knows you, and His first and primary purpose is that you get to know Him and enjoy His love for you. As you open up your life and respond to Him, you will start to discover the unique plan that He has for you. This is confirmed by Paul in his letter to the Ephesians:

'It's in Christ that we find out who we are and what we are living for. Long before we first heard of Christ and got our hopes up, he had his eye on us, had designs on us for glorious living, part of the overall purpose he is working out in everything and everyone.'
(Eph. 1:11, *The Message*)

In other words: God has a dream for you in Christ – for you personally.

Primarily, that dream is for you to have an eternal love-relationship with Him, to become His child, to be loved and to love Him for all eternity. But there is more. God has a purpose for your life that is unique to you, and He wants to reveal it to you.

Your past doesn't disqualify you from living God's dream

You may be thinking that all this talk about God's dream sounds too good to be true. You may be unable to focus on God's plan for your future because you are bogged down by your past, your upbringing, poor choices or your current circumstances. Without realising it, you may be trying to disqualify yourself by constantly looking in the rear-view mirror and focusing on a host of reasons why you will never amount to anything for God. But God doesn't need perfect people with a perfect past. If this was the case, then none of us would qualify! Instead, He loves to take us as we are with all of our flaws and disappointments, and fulfil His wonderful plans in and through us. Joseph is a striking example of that.

On the surface, Joseph had a great start in life. He was the firstborn son of his father's favourite wife, was conceived as a direct result of his mother's answered prayer, and was brought up as his father's favourite son. Yet behind this encouraging report of parental love and God's sovereign power lies a twisted tale of deceit and family dysfunction. Joseph's father, Jacob, aptly named 'deceiver', had infamously cheated his older brother out of his inheritance. Forced to flee from his brother's wrath, Jacob had been packed off to go and find a wife. He met Rachel, fell head over heels in love and received from her father, Laban, a promise of marriage, only to be deceived into first marrying Laban's older, less attractive daughter, Leah.

By the time Joseph was born, Jacob had ten other sons by Leah and two maidservants. Two of Joseph's older brothers, Simeon and Levi, committed mass murder, while his eldest brother had sex with one of his father's wives. To make matters worse, when Joseph was only 12, his mother, Rachel, died giving birth to the youngest son, Benjamin. Bereft of his mother, Joseph grew up as his father's favourite, was given a special coat (which was symbolic of the fact that because he was so special he didn't need to work), and was subsequently hated by his jealous brothers.

So here we have Joseph: a spoilt child, detested by his brothers and with a family history that would have social services working overtime!

However, despite the difficulties surrounding his birth and the trauma yet to come in his life, God's plans and purposes for Joseph remained and God was committed to seeing them fulfilled. Similarly, regardless of how your past or present circumstances have conspired to mess up your life, God *still* has a plan, a purpose and a destiny for you. It may be wise to seek some counselling and healing if your past has been very dysfunctional, but it's also vital to realise the truth that God's plan for your life is still greater than whatever has happened to you in the past. Freed from looking back, you can then start looking forward.

God wants you to dream His dream for your life

If you are going to discover the right dream for your life you must first realise that God has a dream especially for *you*. Joseph didn't wake up one day and think, 'Ah, I need a dream for my life.' No, his dreams *came from God*. Although God is not specifically mentioned here, it is clear from the story as a whole that the narrator intended us to understand that God was the author of this double dream:

> *'Joseph had a dream, and when he told it to his brothers, they hated him all the more. He said to them, "Listen to this dream I had: we were binding sheaves of corn out in the field when suddenly my sheaf rose and stood upright, while your sheaves gathered round mine and bowed down to it." ... Then he had another dream, and he told it to his brothers. "Listen," he said, "I had another dream, and this time the sun and moon and eleven stars were bowing down to me."'*
> (Gen. 37:5–7,9)

You may think, 'I wish it could be that simple for me. I will go to sleep, God will speak to me, give me a blueprint for my life, and that will be that!' But actually, it wasn't that simple for Joseph. What he received from

God was simply a very broad overview of what would happen in his life – of how he was destined to occupy a position of greatness and leadership and how the rest of his family would become subservient to him. That was all he had. It was a true but very incomplete picture of what was about to happen in his life. There was no mention of Egypt or Pharaoh, no mention of famine, no mention of being made a ruler in Egypt – just a simple picture given through two dreams.

At various key junctures in my life I have received a significant 'vision' or 'dream' for the future. When we started the church in Peterborough I had a word from an older man of God saying, 'Think big or you'll limit me.' That was it! There were no further details. But this word helped stir me to believe to see a great church arise in the city. Along the way we received a number of prophetic words and confirmations that we were still on track. Then, after 20 years I had a fresh word. For the first time since we had started in ministry I decided to take a summer study break. On day one, I received a new sense of the Lord's call to start reaching other major cities across the UK, and that we were to begin with Cambridge. Over the following year or so, I received confirming words and pictures from the Lord that, indeed, starting a second centre in Cambridge would be a strategic step in the fulfilment of the rest of the vision.

So – yes, visions and dreams are a crucial way in which God speaks and acts, but it is important to grasp that He is sovereign and, thankfully, He is not limited by our ability to always 'see' and 'hear' things ahead of time! When we do get visions and dreams it is important that we make sure that they are from God and not just the fruit of our desire or imagination. Contrary to the catchy title theme of *Joseph and the Amazing Technicolor Dreamcoat*, any dream *won't* do! Instead, we need a God-dream, a God-vision. We need to connect with what God has conceived and dreamt for our life if we are going to fulfil our destiny and achieve our life's purpose. You may not have been aware until now that God has a dream for you, but He does. The kind of dream we need for our lives is a true God-vision that only comes from the Spirit of God. It is not something we can conceive naturally in our minds. Rather, it is something that the Holy Spirit implants in our hearts. When God 'seeds' an idea in our innermost being and gives us the dream of achieving something, it is entirely different to the kind of dream that arises out of our own imagination. Instead of trying to think up good ideas, we need to connect with the divine destiny that God has decreed for our lives and understand that what He has ordained for us can and will come to pass if we co-operate with Him.

The days of dreams and visions are far from over. In Acts 2:17, Peter (quoting the prophet Joel) says:

'In the last days, God says, I will pour out my Spirit on all people.
Your sons and daughters will prophesy, your young men will see
visions, your old men will dream dreams.'

The Holy Spirit is active in our lives today as the one who reveals God's dreams to us. He wants to speak; He wants to communicate; He wants to show us the purposes God has for our lives. In 1 Corinthians 2:9–10 (NLT), Paul quotes Isaiah: 'No eye has seen, no ear has heard, and no mind has imagined what God has prepared for those who love him' – but God has revealed it to us by His Spirit.

Today, God may still speak to us through dreams, just as He did to Joseph, but there are a number of other ways in which we can begin to hear God's revelation for our lives. We may have a daydream or a waking vision where we see or sense what God is calling us to. At other times God will speak to us through the preaching or prophesying of others as a way of confirming what is already in our hearts and encouraging us to look to larger horizons.

Many times over the years, God has spoken to me simply as I have been reading the Bible. Scriptures are often quickened to me and I have a strong sense that at that moment they are not just God's general, revealed Word for every circumstance, but God's 'now' word to me in a specific situation at a specific time. For example, as we were sensing the Lord's leading to start our new centre in Cambridge, we identified a wonderful facility in which we could start meeting for Sunday services. All seemed to be going well until suddenly, unexpectedly, we began to face some particularly strong opposition to us coming into the area. I was wrestling with anxiety when one morning I 'happened' to be reading Revelation 3 during my daily readings and verses 7–8 just leapt out at me:

> *'These are the words of him who is holy and true, who holds the key of David. What he opens no one can shut, and what he shuts no one can open. I know your deeds. See, I have placed before you an open door that no one can shut.'*

Immediately I took heart. Two days later I heard that the objections had been overcome and we could proceed to signing contracts. God had opened the door that no one would shut. This was not so much hearing God for a new vision, but timely encouragement and confirmation to me that we were on the right track.

Another way to discern what you are called to in life can be through 'holy discontent'. That is, if there is something particularly bothering or troubling you in life, it may be an indication that God is calling you to do something about it. I am not talking about being aggravated by the mundane things that irritate us like traffic jams, or people's headphones being too loud, but about being genuinely troubled by issues in our world such as oppression or injustice. Many a great work or ministry has been started through a 'burden' to see human suffering alleviated. If, for instance, you hate sickness and what it does to people, then it could be that God is calling you into the medical profession or a healing ministry. Some of the most anointed people in the body of Christ who have a ministry of divine healing, have an absolute hatred of sin and sickness and all that it does to people. Maybe there is something in you that hates to see people oppressed, depressed and bound? Maybe there is something about poverty or an area of injustice, perhaps from your own background and experience that God wants to use for your future ministry. It could be that God wants to raise you up and anoint you to be a modern day Joseph: to either exercise significant political influence, or to give you the ability to be successful in business and make money for the kingdom of God, channelling resources in and through the local church into missions and to helping the poor. Examine your heart and discover what you are passionate about. What motivates you? This will be one of the keys to discovering your dream.

One way to tell whether the dream you have is a God-dream (and not something you dreamt up on your own) is to see if it fits in with God's overall counsel in His Word. It's important to ask these questions. Does your dream fit with the truth of the Bible? Does it fit with God's revealed character? Does it fit with His agenda for the Church?

Dreaming God's dream has the power to change your life

There is something powerful about having a dream or vision from God. The Bible says in Proverbs 29:18 that 'Where there is no vision, the people perish' (KJV). In other words, if we lack a vision for our life, it will affect our whole motivation. Without a dream we end up being directionless and easily veer off course in life. Ultimately, this leads to disappointment, frustration and dissatisfaction.

The dream that God gives you, as opposed to any dream you might imagine for yourself, will bring a number of things...

Vision brings passion

Imagine yourself, for a moment, transported to a tropical island in the Caribbean. You are sitting on a largely deserted beach of white sand, enjoying the 27°C heat. A gentle breeze is blowing in from the clear blue ocean and you are sipping a cool drink. You have no agenda other than to take in the view and enjoy the magnificence and beauty of God's creation. Sounds idyllic, doesn't it? Doesn't that scene make you want to be there for real? The fact that we so readily connect with such images tells us something about the way God created us. He enables us to 'see' things in our imagination and visualise what could be. Then, as we begin to desire those things, that vision stirs our emotions. Someone once said, 'There is no such thing as an emotionless vision.' I know exactly what they mean. When God gives us a vision for something it tugs at our emotions. A vision from God makes you come alive! In fact, if in any sense you are feeling somewhat emotionless in your life, it may simply be that you need to reconnect with God's vision for your life. When God speaks to your heart and envisions you, it sparks a passion within you. That passion will propel you forward into your destiny.

It is fairly easy to spot those people who have vision. It is written on their faces and it dictates their actions. Several years ago, our leadership team attended a conference run by a very successful international church ministry. What struck me most was the sheer passion and enthusiasm of their leaders. Here were men and women, some of them well into their fifties, having been involved in ministry for more than thirty years, still oozing vision! I remember thinking, 'These are not people who are ready to be sidelined; these are people burning with a sense of God-destiny and vision. They are living out their dream and yet they know there is much more to come.' Having such a vision produces a passion in our life and causes us to live to see it fulfilled. This then produces motivation.

Vision brings motivation

Sometimes life can be a bit mundane. Vision is the ingredient that changes our motivation in life. I don't know what Mondays are like for you, but I began to love Mondays when I understood the vision God had for me. Why Mondays? Well, on Mondays (often recovering from Sunday!) I sense a new week ahead full of opportunities to see God's purposes further fulfilled. Seeing what lies ahead brings motivation. It helps me to get out of bed each morning and say, 'I know why I am here on this planet.'

Knowing God's dream for our lives will motivate us like nothing else. To be clear, I am not talking about the kind of 'self-motivation' proclaimed by the many self-help or motivational resources on the market. In fact,

I believe that what the world terms 'positive thinking' is actually a distortion of God's truth. It is not simply 'what you believe you can achieve', but knowing that you are fulfilling God's will for your life and are part of His greater purposes that brings the right kind of motivation.

Vision brings direction

Many people live their lives without much sense of direction, and because they lack direction, they are continually blown here and there by their circumstances. Vision, however, brings with it a strong sense of direction. Vision will do for us what blinkers do for a racehorse: stop us from being distracted by peripheral things that would divert us from our goal. It helps us say to ourselves, 'I am not going over there to do that, because I am here doing this!' We can then avoid the pitfall of attempting everything and ending up accomplishing nothing!

Vision brings purpose

Having a vision answers life's most basic question: 'What am I here for?' Every person has an inner belief that they were born for more than they are currently experiencing. Everyone longs to live a life of purpose and meaning that counts for something. All of us, deep down, like to believe that there is some cause, bigger than ourselves, that we are somehow meant to be a part of. There is! I believe this is the cry of the divinely implanted Spirit that urges us to connect with God's dream for our life. Connecting with our vision will give us the sense of purpose and destiny we long for.

Are you ready?

In 1964, one man began quietly buying up land in central Florida, south-west of Orlando, for what he would only term his 'Florida Project'. The project was shrouded in mystery and he set up and used other company names in order to keep it a secret. He acquired around twenty-seven thousand acres of what was essentially wild swampland because he had a dream of building something exceptional.

In October 1971, just seven years later, the doors of Walt Disney World Resort in Orlando, Florida, opened its doors following a special dedication ceremony. Walt Disney himself, the man who dreamed the dream for what is still today the world's largest pleasure resort, had died a few years beforehand in the December of 1966. However, his wife, Lillian, attended the opening to lend her support to the fulfilment of her husband's great project. The Disney Corporation's co-founder and Walt's loyal brother, Roy O. Disney, turned to Lillian at the ceremony and commented privately, 'I wish Walt had lived to see this.' Without hesitation Lillian responded, 'He did, Roy.'

Although I'm sure he would have liked to have been there, in one sense Walt Disney did not need to physically 'see' Disney World come to fruition because he had already seen it. Dreams and visions have incredible power, both in the natural and the spiritual realm. Any business management training programme will teach you that if you don't have a vision for where you are heading you will end up going nowhere. The same is true in your spiritual life.

Remember, though, that you are not called to dream *your* dream, but are called to dream *God's* dream, *His* plan for your life. However, before you can begin living the dream, you are about to discover that you first need to embrace God's preparation – and that is not always easy! Are you ready?

CHAPTER 2

PREPARE TO LIVE THE DREAM

Dreaming the dream is one thing, but living the dream is another matter entirely. Once we have understood something of God's plan for our lives there is invariably a time of preparation before we are ready to walk in the fullness of our destiny. Joseph underwent 13 years of tough training. Moses endured 40 years in the desert. Jesus' disciples were fast-tracked in three and a half years. For each of us the duration may be different, but one thing is clear: we all need to be prepared. While we are undergoing the preparation process it is vital that we hold on to this essential truth: God our Father is good. He loves us, wants the best for us, and is faithfully working out His sovereign purposes in and through us.

My wife Karen and I experienced our own tough preparation during our first four years in Peterborough. We were young, still working on issues in our marriage and learning to parent our six-month-old first daughter, Emily. I was starting a new job school teaching, while finishing a university thesis in holidays and my 'spare time'. In addition, we knew hardly anyone in this totally new city and virtually nothing about church leadership. Then there were the financial pressures. We moved at the height of the property boom in 1988, managed to buy almost the cheapest house on the market (with damp up the walls and rotting windows!), and yet still needed a mortgage that left us regularly praying for extra money to cover basic bills and with virtually no disposable income. We held our first ever church meeting with nine people in this new home on the day that we moved in, with the peeling wallpaper in our dining room providing an interesting backdrop. After a gruelling 18 months, the church had grown to 15 people before experiencing a 'back-door revival' and we went down to six! I was ready to hand my resignation in to the Lord, but He wouldn't accept.

Yet, throughout this season, the Lord was teaching us to put roots deep down in Him at a time when little was showing above ground. We grew closer together as a family, had our second daughter, Annabel, started seeing a small core of people added and experienced miracles of financial provision on a regular basis, often at the eleventh hour. A few years later, I was being prayed for by an older man of God who, while praying, pronounced over me,

'The greater the call, the more radical the surgery!' It wasn't exactly the word I was looking for, but I came to realise that the preparation season, while often tough, had been necessary for what lay ahead.

This was certainly the case with Joseph. His preparation was particularly arduous, but his promotion was spectacular and his later life most fruitful. The psalmist summarised this preparation process:

> *'[God] sent a man before them – Joseph, sold as a slave. They bruised his feet with shackles, his neck was put in irons, till what he foretold came to pass, till the word of the LORD proved him true.'*
> (Psa. 105:17–19)

Like Joseph, each of us has to undergo preparation that is sometimes tough. Thankfully, not everyone has to go through slavery and prison in order to be ready to be used by God! No – He can refine us in the calm as well as in the storm. We shouldn't live hoping for or expecting circumstantial difficulties, thinking that God will only use us if we have been through hardship. Sometimes we go through hardship because we are not prepared to learn an easier way. I have made a decision that I will always try to take the easier route of co-operation with God. I don't want to be stubborn and unreceptive so that He has to teach me everything the hard way. I have seen how, if I keep humbling myself before God, His Word, His Spirit and His people, I can discern His will and walk in it, thereby lightening and shortening the preparation process. This makes the training easier (though not 'easy'), because God does not have to get my attention in a more drastic way.

Nevertheless, there is still a process of preparation, which will usually involve a seeming delay in us living the dream. While waiting, the Scriptures encourage us:

> *'If it [the vision or dream] seems slow in coming, wait. It's on its way. It will come right on time.'* (Hab. 2:3, *The Message*)

I get tested on this all the time. Although I am better than I used to be, I often struggle when it comes to being patient. I don't naturally like waiting! When sitting in a traffic jam, I would much rather find another route a longer way round, rather than sit quietly and patiently. But I have learned that good things come to those who wait and that as I wait expectantly and patiently, the fulfilment of the dream is on its way. It *will* come and it will come in God's time. If right now you are primarily in God's preparation season for your life and are struggling with impatience, realise there are some very important reasons for this seeming 'divine delay'. The first of these is probably the most important...

God is still preparing you

The simple fact is that God loves us too much to promote us before we are ready. It is not so much a matter of our age as our maturity and readiness to handle the inevitable blessings and pressures that elevation will bring to our lives. Although it's not easy, we have to learn not to try to force the pace, allowing God to do His work in us in His time. As we wait patiently, God uses that time to deal with character weaknesses that could later cause great harm to ourselves or others if left unchecked.

As we look carefully at the character of Joseph, the 17-year-old dreamer, it becomes quite clear that he was not mature enough to fulfil his destiny, which would ultimately include having to lead an entire nation. From the start of the narrative, we clearly see that here was a young man with some serious character flaws. While keeping the flock with his brothers, for instance, the Bible records that he went back to their father and brought him a 'bad report' about them (Gen. 37:2). This was not just an instance of a childish 'tell-tale' attitude, but an indication of a judgmental and self-seeking character. Joseph's father had probably not helped the situation by showing obvious favouritism to his son, bestowing on him the gift of a tunic of many colours. Nevertheless, Joseph was responsible for his own attitude of prideful superiority.

Further evidence of character deficiencies are revealed in the way he responded to his dreams. The Scriptures record how:

'Joseph had a dream, and when he told it to his brothers, they hated him all the more ... Then he had another dream, and he told it to his brothers.' (Gen. 37:5,9)

His enthusiastic telling of the dreams to his brothers – especially since they pictured the rest of the family subjugated to Joseph in some way – reveals a distinct lack of wisdom. Not least because he must have known his brothers were already jealous of him and hated him. Now he is unwisely speaking about how he will be lifted up above them! Moreover, he told his brothers not once, but twice. It doesn't take a lot of imagination to realise that this must have gone down like a lead balloon! Clearly it matters a lot what we do with what God tells us. It may not be wise to go around telling people that we're going to be the next Billy Graham, Winston Churchill or Nelson Mandela.

Joseph not only lacked wisdom, he also had a pride problem. This was very serious because the Scriptures make clear that pride comes before a fall (Prov. 18:12). It was at the heart of Lucifer's rebellion and is the antithesis of joyful submission to God, who 'opposes the proud, but gives grace to the humble' (James 4:6, NLT). God knew, of course, that Joseph had a pride problem before He gave him the dream. He also knew that pride would have to be dealt with. This is probably the main reason for the length and seriousness of Joseph's preparation.

Looking back at our own preparation season in the early days in Peterborough, the Lord certainly used that time to deal with pride in my life. Having been used to succeeding in many areas of life, it felt as if I was failing, and failing badly. I came to the point where I realised that I couldn't build the church in my own strength. I couldn't just 'make things happen'. I had to come to a point of total reliance on the Lord for the grace, anointing, wisdom and strategy to see *His* Church established. I had to learn – and am still learning – that if I try to initiate something out of my own desire or impatience, without waiting on Him for the right idea, personnel and timing – then invariably I will mess up what He is trying to do.

If pride is so dangerous, we need to be aware that often its main root in our lives is insecurity. Our lack of security in God and who we are in Christ can open the door to pride. Insecurity and its accompanying feelings can fuel prideful and arrogant behaviour to 'protect' ourselves. Insecurity makes us feel that we have to let everyone know who we are and what we've accomplished. But it is based on a lie. No matter how impressive our dreams or achievements, they are not what makes us 'who we are'. Instead, we need to grow deeper in our security in God and resist all fear, inferiority, insecurity and pride.

Whatever areas we need to grow in, God is merciful and wants to work *in* us to a deeper level, before working *through* us in a greater way. If we walk with Him and submit to His dealings in our lives, we can be assured that He won't allow us to be promoted too early, or give us more than we can handle.

God is still refining the dream in you

There is a second reason for a 'divine delay'. If you have received what you believe is a vision or dream from God for your future, then realise that it is probably only a partial picture of what is to come. The apostle Paul makes clear that even in the post-Pentecost age, when the Holy Spirit has been poured out on the Church, 'we know in part and we prophesy in part' (1 Cor. 13:9). In other words, rarely does God show us the whole picture for our lives all at once. If He did reveal to us now the full magnitude of His will for our life and all we will have to go through in order to see it fulfilled, we would probably not be able to handle it. So instead, like creating a painting, God gives us a broad impression of what will become and then slowly but surely fills in the detail. We may be aware of Him painting in some of the background, adding a touch of colour here and there, but there is still a whole aspect of the picture we have yet to see. We need to be patient while God works to bring the whole dream to completion.

However, not only is our seeing of *what* God has in store for us usually incomplete, but our understanding of the full reason *why* God is calling us is often unclear. This concerns the vital issue of our *motivation*. At age 17, Joseph, like many teenagers (and many beyond their teens), probably thought that he was the centre of the universe. The prospect of being elevated above his brothers clearly pandered to his youthful pride. It took many years for him to grasp a more mature understanding of God's plan for his life. Having been betrayed by his brothers but elevated by God, years later Joseph was able to reflect on the events of his life and reassure them with these amazing words:

> *'do not be distressed and do not be angry with yourselves for selling me here, because it was to save lives that God sent me ahead of you … God sent me … to preserve for you a remnant on earth and to save your lives by a great deliverance. So then, it was not you who sent me here, but God.'*
> (Gen. 45:5,7–8)

Later, in Genesis 50:20, he says again:

> *'You intended to harm me, but God intended it all for good. He brought me to this position so I could save the lives of many people.'*
> (NLT)

Eventually, Joseph came to realise that his greatness was not primarily about him and his destiny, but about God's great plan to save the lives of others and to change their destiny. Put simply, Joseph was elevated so that God's mighty purposes might be fulfilled. These plans involved nothing less than the salvation from starvation of the whole of the Near East, as well as the preservation of God's chosen people.

Maybe you have had a word from God and thought, 'Wow, I'm God's answer!' If so, like Joseph, you need to let the dream mature in you.

God is not interested in exalting you just so you can feel better about yourself. He has a greater purpose for your life. The apostle Paul put it very simply when he said:

'It is God himself who made us what we are and given us new lives from Christ Jesus; and long ages ago he planned that we should spend these lives in helping others.' (Eph. 2:10, TLB)

This helps us understand God's agenda. If, at present, your destiny only has you in the picture, then it is an 'in part' vision. It is important to come to the realisation that, while fulfilling you in the process, God wants to raise you up to help others. It's that simple.

I know when we were first called to Peterborough that the vision we had received was prophetic but partial. First, we were given a word to, 'think big or you'll limit me', which in effect helped us become aware that God had big plans for us. Years later, however, when the church had begun to grow, we sensed the vision maturing in us. Instead of focusing on 'numbers' we began to place a greater emphasis on God's work in the lives of individuals. Our focus shifted from building a big church, to building 'big people' – which of course, in turn, would lead to a large, healthy church. This shift in vision was encapsulated in a new mission statement: *Transforming lives from our neighbourhoods to the nations by the power of God's love.*

Since then, God's vision for our future has continued to unfold, with a clear sense that we are being called to play our part – together with many other great churches and ministries – to see the gospel of Jesus preached in cities and regions across the UK and into other nations. This maturing of the vision has been a vital part of us stepping into our destiny.

God is still working on the circumstances around you

Not only do we have to let the dream mature in us, but we have to realise that there are people and circumstances around us that need to be in place for the dream to be fulfilled. God knows the plan ahead of time and is orchestrating situations both in our lives and in the lives of others to get things ready. The time will come when all the elements necessary have fallen into place and the vision is ready to be fulfilled. God alone sees the whole picture and so we need to submit both to His ways and His timing.

God not only needed to prepare Joseph during the 13-year trial, but He was also preparing the circumstances ready for his elevation. Even if Joseph himself had been 'ready' at 17 when he received his dream, the wider situation was not. Joseph's breakthrough moment would have to coincide with the desperate need of the day. To arrive at the right place at the right time, he would experience a series of providentially ordered circumstances and connections: going to Egypt, ending up in prison, meeting Pharaoh's servants, interpreting their dreams, being released from prison, and interpreting Pharaoh's dreams of future prosperity and famine. Only then could he be in place to save his own family and the future people of God, as well as saving Egypt from starvation. 'Cometh the hour, cometh the man!'

You may have heard God correctly about your own future, but realise that He is simply giving you an 'ahead-of-time' perspective so that you have time to prepare. God rarely reveals to us something that is supposed to happen 'today'. This may sometimes happen with the small details of our lives, but rarely with regard to His bigger purposes.

One reason why we can often become confused about what God has said is not that we have necessarily heard incorrectly, but we have failed to understand His timing. We naturally want things to happen sooner rather than later. I am learning that if God is the author of the vision, He is the one who is going to give the power to see it come to pass. My job, therefore, is to wait for His timing. If I get the right thing in the right way but at the wrong time, it will still be wrong! In some of my more frustrated moments over the years I have said to the Lord, 'God, this is moving so slowly!' and very often He has responded to me by saying, 'You're on a pace to match my grace!'

How do we respond?

Although the preparation season is a time where we have to wait to see God's vision for our life fulfilled, it is certainly not a time to sit on our hands and do nothing, simply waiting for something 'big' to happen. That's not the way it works. Joseph's spectacular promotion as second-in-command to the Egyptian pharaoh, was not accomplished by simply waiting, but by working hard and serving in slavery and prison years before his breakthrough came. We, too, must continue to work faithfully *where we are right now*, with the level of resources and wisdom that God has given us, knowing that as we are faithful with little, promotion is on the way!

During this training period, it is important that we don't get discouraged or distracted. Like a runner in a race, we are to throw off everything that would hinder us, fixing our eyes on Jesus who has gone before us (Heb. 12:1–3). We are to embrace God's preparation as a good thing. In the words of the writer of the Hebrews:

> 'So don't feel sorry for yourselves. Or have you forgotten how good parents treat children, and that God regards you as his children? My dear child, don't shrug off God's discipline, but don't be crushed by it either. It's the child he loves that he disciplines; the child he embraces, he also corrects. God is educating you; that's why you must never drop out. He's treating you as dear children. This trouble you're in isn't punishment; it's training, the normal experience of children. Only irresponsible parents leave children to fend for themselves. Would you prefer an irresponsible God? We respect our own parents for training

*and not spoiling us, so why not embrace God's training so we can truly
live? While we were children, our parents did what seemed best to
them. But God is doing what is best for us, training us to live God's holy
best. At the time, discipline isn't much fun. It always feels like it's going
against the grain. Later, of course, it pays off handsomely, for it's the
well-trained who find themselves mature in their relationship with God.'*
(Heb. 12:5–11, *The Message*)

Such preparation is essential for right promotion. Any *Star Wars* fan
will recall the scene from *The Empire Strikes Back* in which the young,
headstrong Jedi Knight, Luke Skywalker, wants to set out to rescue his
friends Han Solo and Princess Leia. Luke knows he has 'the Force' and
he knows his friends are in trouble, so he wants to end his Jedi training
prematurely and go to help them. Luke's mentors, Obi Wan Kenobi and
Yoda, try to persuade him that the most important thing is for him to
complete his preparation. Then, and only then, will he be ready to face
the dangers that lie ahead. Skywalker decides to cut the preparation short
and go and rescue his friends anyway, and because this is Hollywood,
somehow everything works out OK! But in this galaxy, in real life, there
are no short cuts. We need to complete God's training programme so that
He can entrust us with all He has for us.

CHAPTER 3

OVERCOMING OFFENCES

During his 13-year preparation period, Joseph had to face three primary tests. These concerned the need for forgiveness, faithfulness and fruitfulness. The forgiveness test – the focus of this chapter – was arguably the greatest of the three, because Joseph had more than his share of opportunities to get offended. Yet, it was his ability to forgive that marked him out as a shining example for subsequent generations. Well-known authors have picked up on this theme of forgiveness as being central to the whole Joseph story. R.T. Kendall, in his book *God Meant It For Good*, identifies 'total forgiveness' as a primary lesson from the life of Joseph. Similarly, Charles Swindoll, in his book *Joseph: A Man of Integrity and Forgiveness*, writes:

> *'Here is one on the list of God's 'greats' ... a life lived ... high above the all-too-common reactions of rage, resentment and revenge. Here is one who deliberately chose to overlook unfair offences, to overcome enormous obstacles, and model a virtue that is fast becoming lost in our hostile age – forgiveness.'*[1]

The significance of passing the forgiveness test is huge. If you and I want to live the dream, it is essential that we live free from offence. Nothing will block us from realising our dream more effectively than unforgiveness, bitterness and resentment.

A few years ago, some good friends of ours from Los Angeles told me about the findings of a Christian psychologist, Dr Fred Gross. As director of three clinics, he had ministered to more than nineteen thousand people over a 30-year period. His patients had suffered from all kinds of conditions ranging from emotional turmoil to depression, suicide, breakdown and mental illness. The one common denominator was unforgiveness.

Unforgiveness is, as we shall see, a spiritual problem, but it has catastrophic consequences in every area of our lives: mentally, emotionally and sometimes physically too. I remember early in our married life, during the first period of our ministry in Peterborough, Karen suffered from intense pain in her lower back. We did everything we knew to do: we prayed for healing, we anointed with oil, but nothing seemed to work. Then the Lord revealed that the root of the problem wasn't actually physical at all. In the course of church work, someone had said something hurtful to Karen, which she had held onto. That hurt led to an emotional wound, which had manifested itself in the pain in her back. Once we had identified the source of the problem, she forgave the person and immediately her back was healed.

I remember a similar scenario with a member of the congregation. She was unable to move her neck, which was in a brace. In one particular church meeting she came forward in response to a call to deal with any issues of unforgiveness. Having repented and forgiven the person in question, she returned to her seat. As she sat down, the person sitting behind her called her name and, without thinking, she turned round to respond to them. At that moment she discovered that her neck had been completely healed. No one had prayed specifically for her to be healed. She had simply dealt with her unforgiveness and as a result her body was restored to health.

We need to realise that we are integrated beings, comprising spirit, soul and body (1 Thess. 5:23). If we are wounded in one area, that wound can affect the other areas, and probably the greatest damage and bondage in our lives comes through harbouring unforgiveness and resentment towards others. This chapter, then, is vital for your health! We must look in more detail at the offences that came to Joseph and examine his responses. The first thing we need to establish is that...

Offences do come

The reality of life is that other people will offend us, regularly! While this is not good news, it is a fact of living in a fallen world. For Joseph, especially in his late teens and early twenties, the offences came thick and fast and can be categorised into three major areas. The first was, arguably, the most serious.

Rejection and abuse

In Acts 7:9, Stephen reminds his listeners: 'Because the patriarchs were jealous of Joseph, they sold him as a slave into Egypt.' Behind this simple summary lies a long history of resentment and rejection. Although he was loved as his father's favourite to the point of being spoilt, Joseph's favouritism marked him as the odd one out and made him the object of his brothers' jealousy. His special coat, intended as a sign of blessing from Jacob, in fact led to rejection by his brothers; so much so that they 'hated him and could not speak a kind word to him' (Gen. 37:4). Children and teenagers can be very cruel and one can only imagine the sense of pain that this rejection had on the young Joseph at such a formative time in his life. For Joseph, the situation got much worse after he had 'shared' his dream with the family. The writer of Genesis records the reaction of the brothers to his first dream:

> '"Do you intend to reign over us? Will you actually rule us?" And they hated him all the more because of his dream and what he had said.'
> (Gen. 37:8)

After hearing about the second dream, their hatred developed into a seething jealousy (Gen. 37:11) and simmering resentment, which reached boiling point when Joseph was sent by his father to go and check up on his brothers who were grazing the flocks. The writer records:

> 'they saw him in the distance, and before he reached them, they plotted to kill him. "Here comes that dreamer!" they said to each other. "Come now, let's kill him and throw him into one of these cisterns and say that a ferocious animal devoured him. Then we'll see what comes of his dreams." ... So when Joseph came to his brothers, they stripped him of his robe – the ornate robe he was wearing – and they took him and threw him into the cistern.' (Gen. 37:18–20,23–24)

Verbal and emotional abuse now manifested itself in full-blown physical abuse. The language seems to be deliberately violent: 'Come now, let's kill him and throw him ... they stripped him of his robe ... they took him and threw him'. How devastating and humiliating to be stripped and left helpless in a pit. Yet God was watching over Joseph. Instead of killing him, the brothers decided to sell him to some Ishmaelite traders for 20 shekels of silver. They then slaughtered a goat, took Joseph's robe and dipped it in the blood. They took the tunic back to their distraught father with the story that his favourite son had been killed by a ferocious animal. Meanwhile, the Ishmaelites took Joseph to Egypt where he was sold as a slave to Potiphar, one of Pharaoh's officials, the captain of the guard. Joseph had been suddenly demoted from being his father's favourite to being a slave in a foreign country. Such violent rejection, betrayal and abuse foreshadowed the greater suffering of Jesus. He was rejected by His fellow Jews, betrayed, sold for 30 pieces of silver, stripped, cruelly tortured and then actually killed as a substitute for us.

Let's pause and ponder what Joseph went through. While chronicling these events, the narrator simply relays the facts and doesn't include any material that might give us insight into Joseph's response. Later, however, we get the report of the brothers who guiltily recall, 'We saw how distressed he was when he pleaded with us for his life, but we would not listen' (Gen. 42:21). Here is a young, vulnerable 17-year-old being physically abused and nearly killed by his own brothers. Man's inhumanity to man was as shocking then as it is now. Whether it manifests itself in individual acts of murder, rape or abuse, or in national acts of genocide, sadly such hatred still continues. It may be that you have experienced such rejection and even abuse, either emotionally, physically or sexually. If that is true then please know this: first, that there is healing available to you in Christ, through the path of forgiveness; second, that no circumstance that has conspired to defeat you can terminate the plans and purpose of God for your life.

False accusation and unjust punishment

As if being rejected, abused, nearly killed and sold into slavery by his brothers was not enough, Joseph would now experience false accusation and unjust punishment of the most severe kind. In the next chapter we will deal more fully with the issue of temptation as Joseph faced a full-on seduction from Potiphar's wife. But for now we note that having successfully and repeatedly resisted her advances, she vengefully turns on him, falsely accusing him of rape, first to the household servants and then her husband:

> *'That Hebrew slave ... came to me to make sport of me. But as soon as I screamed for help, he left his cloak beside me and ran out of the house.'* (Gen. 39:17–18)

Of course, this is the exact opposite of the truth. She had totally twisted the facts and slandered Joseph to protect her own reputation. The normal response to false accusation is self-justification, but there is no record of Joseph attempting to defend himself. Given that he was a Hebrew slave in a foreign land it may have made matters worse. Potiphar chooses to believe his wife and in his anger, throws Joseph into prison. (As an aside, some commentators say it's likely that Potiphar didn't actually believe his wife. If he had believed that Joseph was trying to rape her, he probably would have had him killed. Instead, in an act of 'mercy' he promptly put him in prison.) This unjust accusation and punishment was, nevertheless, a bitter pill to swallow. We never hear of Joseph being cleared of that rape charge. Moreover, he 'lost' a decade or so of his prime youth suffering in an Egyptian prison – all because he took a stand for righteousness. Yet, amazingly, there is no record of him allowing bitterness or self-pity to grip his soul.

It may be that you have been a victim of false accusation and that, like Joseph, it has cost you much. But take heart and look at Joseph. He passed the test, forgave his accusers and like Jesus, centuries later, came out in triumph.

Unfairly forgotten and overlooked

The third major offence came after Joseph had already been in prison for many years. He found himself in the company of two of the king's servants, the cupbearer and the baker. Both men had dreams they didn't understand and Joseph was able to faithfully interpret the meaning of their dreams. To one of these men, the cupbearer, he prophesied restoration, before exhorting him with the following words: 'But when all goes well with you, remember me and show me kindness; mention me to Pharaoh and get me out of this prison' (Gen. 40:14). Sometime later, having been restored, it is recorded simply and starkly that the cupbearer 'did not remember Joseph; he forgot him' (Gen. 40:23). This neglect was very costly, resulting in Joseph spending another two years in prison. The writer hints at how tough this must have been, describing this time as 'two *full* years' (Gen. 41:1, my emphasis).

Have you ever been overlooked? Maybe your parents always seemed to prefer your sibling over you? Maybe you should have received a promotion at work but somebody else got it instead? Maybe there was a ministry position in your church that you desperately wanted, but it was given to someone else and not you? If so, then be encouraged by the story of Joseph. His suffering was particularly severe. It was not simply that his feelings were hurt; rather he spent two extra years in an Egyptian prison – all because someone forgot about him. But God didn't forget Joseph. And He will not forget you.

You can overcome offences

So here we have a catalogue of very serious offences, spread across a 13-year period. But the wonderful news is that although offences came to Joseph, they did not overcome him. Rather, he overcame them. So can you and I. Centuries later, as he recounted the history of Israel, Stephen reminded his hearers of the trials of Joseph and how they ended in triumph: 'But God was with him and rescued him from all his troubles' (Acts 7:9–10).

The fact that 'God was with him' was both the key to his ability to forgive and a clear indicator that he had been forgiven.

That Joseph did forgive his oppressors is clear enough. Exactly when and how is less obvious. R.T. Kendall argues that Joseph stayed in prison for the length of time he did, including the final 'two full years', because he had not practised *total forgiveness*. To support his case, Kendall highlights Joseph's request to the cupbearer to remember him before Pharaoh, where he added, 'I was forcibly carried off from the land of the Hebrews, and even here I have done nothing to deserve being put in a dungeon' (Gen 40:15). However, whether this represents a lack of total forgiveness or is simply a statement of fact, is unclear.

So what evidence do we have to draw a conclusion either way? In the early years the evidence is largely one of silence, since the narrator doesn't give us an inside look at Joseph's reactions or emotions during the crises of the pit, the palace or the prison. Yet, the striking and frequently recorded phrase 'the LORD was with him' (Gen. 39:2,3,21; Acts 7:9) suggests that in both the Old and New Testament, Joseph is presented as a righteous man who was fully vindicated by the Lord from his largely unjust suffering. As a result of the Lord's presence with him, not only did Joseph prosper as a slave and a prisoner, but those around him took notice and promoted him accordingly. It is therefore reasonable to assume, from the evidence of the rest of the Bible and the New Testament in particular, that somehow and in a considerable measure, Joseph did find the grace to forgive and move on.

In Hebrews 12:15, for example, bitterness and resentment is presented as something dangerous that will cause harm to many:

'See to it that no one falls short of the grace of God and that no bitter root grows up to cause trouble and defile many.'

In Joseph's case, in spite of the huge offences that he endured, the overwhelming evidence is that the grace and favour of God was still very much in evidence in his life, even if the completion of his season of preparation was still some way off. Therefore, the strong implication is that he did manage to exercise forgiveness, thereby enabling the grace of God to flow in and through his life.

So, what then are we to make of the long dramatic interplay with his brothers in Egypt several years later (Gen. 42–45)? We will cover this in some detail in Chapters 8 and 9. But for now it is sufficient to acknowledge that at first glance it seems as if Joseph was exploiting the situation, using the fact that he now had power over his brothers, deliberately concealing his identity, while seemingly enjoying their discomfort and distress. Yet, as we shall see, there was probably another more important reason why Joseph was 'testing' them as he did. Even if he had forgiven them before God, he still needed to see if they had come to a place of repentance before trusting them enough to be reconciled to them. This is a crucial point: forgiveness is one thing, relational reconciliation is another.

I would strongly suggest that Joseph was able, before God, to forgive his brothers 'in his heart' years prior to re-encountering them. The fact that he did meant that God was able to prosper him during his preparation, and then dramatically promote him before Pharaoh. Without having forgiven, he would not have been free to live the dream. The same is true for us today, except that we have a huge advantage over Joseph: Jesus has come both as an example and as a substitute for us. So if Joseph could forgive then, we can certainly do so now.

Many years ago, Joseph's example was hugely helpful for me. I was in my early twenties and had temporarily been given leadership of a small church near Oxford. I was completely inexperienced and out of my depth, having only been a Christian for a few years. Only a few months into this new role, one Sunday morning an older Christian and long-standing member of the congregation came up to me after I had preached and told me in no uncertain terms that there were a number of things lacking in my leadership of the church. He was probably right, but my reaction was all wrong. Having just preached my heart out, and doing the best job that I knew how, I remember beginning to feel seriously hurt and offended. After the meeting I went on a walk with Karen around the grounds of Blenheim Palace and began replaying and rehearsing the incident, only to find that the more I talked the worse I felt! But help was on the way. I had been listening to some teaching on the importance of forgiveness and the Lord spoke to me and reminded me of the example of Joseph: how he had been able to forgive and how, rather than allowing his offences to become his *stumbling block*, they became his *stepping stone* into God's destiny. I decided that I wanted nothing to stop me moving forward in His plans, so I was able to forgive the church member and received peace and freedom once more.

The crucial importance of forgiving others is a central part of Jesus' teaching. In the Lord's Prayer, for example, He instructed His disciples to pray, 'forgive us our debts, as we also have forgiven our debtors' (Matt. 6:12). Then, as if to highlight the central importance of this particular part of the prayer, He concludes with the following sobering words:

> 'For if you forgive other people when they sin against you, your
> heavenly Father will also forgive you. But if you do not forgive others
> their sins, your Father will not forgive your sins.' (Matt. 6:14–15)

The clear message here is that horizontal unforgiveness towards other human beings will block us from receiving vertical forgiveness from God the Father. Jesus is, in effect, saying that if we don't get this matter of forgiving others sorted out then it will block our relationship with our Father, and therefore all other forms of prayer will not work for us. Furthermore, in the parable of the unmerciful servant in Matthew 18, Jesus highlights the fact that unforgiveness has a binding effect on all concerned.

The apostle Paul makes a similarly serious point. In Ephesians 4:25–5:2, he stresses the importance of keeping right attitudes and maintaining right relationships, thereby not giving the devil a foothold (v27), nor grieving the Holy Spirit of God who lives within (v30). While this passage is clearly not speaking about the loss of eternal salvation (since we are by the Spirit 'sealed for the day of redemption' (v30)), it does emphasise how unresolved anger can open the door to the devil and how our bad attitudes towards others greatly hinder our walk with God's Spirit. With this in mind, we are instructed to deal radically with all forms of offence and unforgiveness:

> *'Get rid of all bitterness, rage and anger, brawling and slander, along with every form of malice. Be kind and compassionate to one another, forgiving each other, just as in Christ God forgave you. Follow God's example, therefore, as dearly loved children and live a life of love, just as Christ loved us and gave himself up for us as a fragrant offering and sacrifice to God.'* (Eph. 4:31–5:2)

This vital passage highlights three important principles that help us in the whole area of forgiveness: a) God has forgiven us through the sacrifice of Christ, b) we must forgive others as God has forgiven us, and c) we must live a life of love. Let's look at each of these in turn...

God has forgiven us in Christ

Paul emphasises that the sacrifice of Christ is the basis for all true and total forgiveness. In Ephesians 4:32 he uses the phrase, 'just as in Christ God forgave you' and then in similar terms in 5:2, states, 'just as Christ loved us and gave himself up for us as a fragrant offering and sacrifice to God'. Unlike Joseph, we have the benefit of being able to look back to the cross of Christ as both our source and inspiration for forgiving others.

In the parable of the unmerciful servant, Jesus highlights how great the debt that we have been forgiven is, depicted as 'ten thousand talents' (Matt. 18:24, KJV). In my own experience, being reminded of how much I have been forgiven – the fact that I have been released totally from an unpayable debt – helps hugely in extending forgiveness to others. This is particularly so when it comes to matters where the offence may seem particularly serious or painful. Knowing that instead of judgment I have received mercy, helps me to take the second step, which is to...

Forgive others as I have been forgiven

Paul's twice repeated phrase 'just as' emphasises the link between God's forgiveness and our forgiving others. *The Message* translation of Ephesians 4:32 brings out the meaning nicely:

> *'Forgive one another as quickly and thoroughly as God in Christ forgave you.'*

I remember that, when our two daughters were growing up, we attempted to teach them the notion of unconditional forgiveness. If they were naughty we would discipline them, let the tears take their natural course and then would hug, kiss and be reconciled, and would frequently say these words over them: 'It's forgiven, forgotten, gone!' But not only are we to forgive quickly and thoroughly when being offended, we are to go 'on the offensive' and...

Walk in love

I remember years ago as a young Christian learning that rather than just waiting to forgive others (reactively) when they offended me, I needed to take a further step of deciding *in advance* to forgive people and walk in love, even before I had been offended. So, when it came to praying the forgiveness part of the Lord's Prayer, I did three things: 1) I asked the Lord to shine His light into my heart, and asked for His forgiveness where I had sinned against Him; 2) I forgave and released anyone who had offended me; and 3) I prayed at the start of my day that I would forgive anyone who might sin against me. And it worked! I found that having decided beforehand to forgive before any offences had been committed, I was able to forgive 'on the go', without allowing offences to take root, and that is definitely the best and easiest way.

The decision to forgive

This is good news! We don't need to be overcome by offences, but we can overcome them. In fact, it is vital that we live a life of forgiveness if we want to walk in God's plan for our lives. So, my question is, *who do you need to forgive?* Do you have any unresolved issues relating to others? If you have been rejected and abused, particularly when you were younger and especially by those closest to you, then the wounds may still be deep and painful. If you have experienced false accusation and unjust punishment, especially if you are still suffering the consequences, then it can be really tough to handle. If you have been neglected, overlooked, passed over or forgotten and maybe are still in a period of 'delayed blessing' as a result, then you may be struggling to deal with the feelings of resentment. If so, then make a decision to forgive. If necessary, pray with a friend (without dishonouring the person who has offended you) or get together with a church leader to help you move on.

As you do, take comfort from Joseph. He endured all of these hardships and yet, somehow, hundreds of years prior to Christ coming, found a grace to forgive and move on. As a result 'the Lord was with him' and 'he prospered'. Now, post-Calvary, we have the benefit of being recipients of His unconditional and total forgiveness. For this reason we certainly have the power to forgive and be free!

CHAPTER 4

TRIUMPHING OVER TEMPTATION

We live in a culture that seems obsessed with sex. Moreover, sexual activity is celebrated, encouraged or tolerated in ways that are far removed from the God-given boundaries of sex within a faithful marriage between a husband and wife (see Gen. 2:23–25; Eph. 5:22–33). For young people and not-so-young people today, standing against this tide of sexual immorality is one of the biggest tests of faithfulness to the Lord and His Word. Yet, it is a test that each of us must pass if we are to walk in God's plan for our lives. This chapter is designed to strengthen such a resolve without condemning those who have already 'fallen' and are in need of forgiveness, cleansing and restoration.

The good news is that you can stand! That is the stunning lesson from the life of Joseph. This young man, isolated in the seductive world of ancient Egypt, succeeded in resisting full-on sexual seduction and as a result moved on into God's plan for his life. Having taken and passed the forgiveness test, he successfully navigated his way through the dangerous waters of sexual temptation. In Genesis 37 we see Joseph in Canaan, dreaming, being betrayed and sold in to slavery. In chapter 39 the scene has shifted to Egypt. There, having risen to prominence within Potiphar's household, Joseph faced arguably his greatest test:

'Now Joseph was well-built and handsome, and after a while his master's wife took notice of Joseph and said, "Come to bed with me!" But he refused. "With me in charge," he told her, "my master does not concern himself with anything in the house; everything he owns he has entrusted to my care. No one is greater in this house than I am. My master has withheld nothing from me except you, because you are his wife. How then could I do such a wicked thing and sin against God?" And though she spoke to Joseph day after day, he refused to go to bed with her or even to be with her. One day he went into the house to attend to his duties, and none of the household servants was inside. She caught him by his cloak and said, "Come to bed with me!" But he left his cloak in her hand and ran out of the house. When she saw that he had left his cloak in her hand and had run

out of the house, she called her household servants. "Look," she said
to them, "this Hebrew has been brought to us to make sport of us!
He came in here to sleep with me, but I screamed. When he heard me
scream for help, he left his cloak beside me and ran out of the house."
She kept his cloak beside her until his master came home. Then she
told him this story: "That Hebrew slave you brought us came to me
to make sport of me. But as soon as I screamed for help, he left his
cloak beside me and ran out of the house." When his master heard the
story his wife told him, saying, "This is how your slave treated me,"
he burned with anger. Joseph's master took him and put him in prison,
the place where the king's prisoners were confined.' (Gen. 39:6–20)

This stunning picture of Joseph's refusal to compromise his moral integrity and faithfulness to the Lord stands out in direct contrast to the adulterous scheming of his older brother Judah in Genesis 38. It is as if the narrator is highlighting that here, in Joseph, is a man of sufficient character and self-discipline who could be used as a mighty leader in God's sovereign purposes.

For us, too, if we want to fully live God's dream for our lives, we have much to learn from Joseph. Some of the following nine principles are directly related to Joseph's victory.[2] Others are applicable to us as New Testament believers with greater resources at our disposal than were available to Joseph and other Old Testament saints. The fact remains that if Joseph could overcome, then you and I can certainly do so. First, when tempted, we need to...

Reject intimidation

Many times sincere Christians immediately go on the back foot because they feel insecure and intimidated, simply because they are being tempted. But it is vital that you stay on the front foot and don't give in to such feelings. If you're being tempted right now it's not necessarily a sign of weakness or spiritual immaturity, it may just be an indication that you are, at this time, a particular target of the devil.

There is a big difference between temptation and giving in to the temptation. In the memorable words of the great sixteenth-century reformer, Martin Luther, 'You can't stop the birds flying over your head, but you can stop them building a nest in your hair.' For example, it is one thing to receive a tempting thought to go and look at pornography on the internet, but quite another to actually go online and indulge. You can't always stop these thoughts coming in the first place, but you can stop yourself dwelling on them, receiving them, and acting on them either in your mind, your heart or with your body. So don't be discouraged if you're being tempted right now. Like Joseph, you can find a way out and live the dream that God has for you.

So don't be intimidated! Every single person who has ever lived has faced temptation in some way: Adam and Eve, Abraham, Moses, David, Solomon and even Jesus, the Son of God. The only difference between Jesus and any other human being on the planet today is that Jesus faced temptation but never sinned. Sometimes we can be deceived into thinking that we are unique in facing a particularly testing onslaught. But Paul reassures us that the opposite is true:

'No temptation has overtaken you except what is common to mankind. And God is faithful; he will not let you be tempted beyond what you can bear. But when you are tempted, he will also provide a way out so that you can endure it.' (1 Cor. 10:13)

This is extremely encouraging! If temptation is Satan's age-old strategy to derail you, then your Father will not let you be tempted beyond what you can stand, and has planned a way of escape for you.

If rejecting intimidation is the first step, the second is somewhat contrasting...

Realise your vulnerability

This is vital, because to be forewarned is to be forearmed. The apostle Paul warns us against complacency: 'So, if you think you are standing firm, be careful that you don't fall!' (1 Cor. 10:12). Realising your vulnerability doesn't mean that you prepare to give in, but rather that you are more alert to deal with the temptation when it comes. Hopefully the following study of the 'what', 'when', 'why', 'where' and 'how' of temptation will help forearm you.

What?

The three major and most common areas of temptation are pride, money and sex. Sadly, history is littered with those who have succumbed to one or more of these big three. Part of the reason why so many are defeated in these areas is because Satan has deceived people about the essential nature and goodness of God. Genesis 1–3 makes it abundantly clear that God is good and the author of everything good, while Satan is the one who perverts and distorts. God created this whole world and gave mankind authority to rule over it and enjoy it. Therefore, He is not against us having authority and influence. He is not against us having money or enjoying the good things of life. He is not against us enjoying sex. What He is against is us lusting after things illegitimately, placing them before obedience to His will. This is where the devil's deception comes in.

While all three areas of pride, money and sex are important, the focus of this chapter is on sexual temptation, partly because this was the primary test that Joseph faced here in Genesis 39 (we will look at his handling of 'influence' and 'affluence' in Chapter 6), but also because it is such a major challenge in our culture today. One only has to channel hop through the TV, be online, glance at newspaper racks or magazine stands, or simply listen to conversations in the workplace or during leisure time, to know that sexual temptation is all around us. Tragically, it is often the one area rarely or never talked about in church, so believers are often unprepared for the challenge.

The purpose of this chapter is not to point a big finger, however, but to help strengthen you by the Word of God to overcome in this crucial area. As we focus specifically on sexual temptation, it is very helpful to be aware of the following question...

When?

We need to realise that we are more vulnerable at certain times than at others. I think Joseph was doubly vulnerable at the time of his temptation. On the one hand, he was in a season of great success. The Lord was evidently with him and he was prospering – so much so that he was given huge influence and responsibility over Potiphar's household. So too we can be most vulnerable at times when life seems to be going well and spiritual complacency can set in.

On the other hand, Joseph was also tempted in a time of real weakness. Here he was, a young, single man, away from his home and family, a slave in a foreign culture, and he is confronted with a persistent, full-on offer of sex. Sometimes the most vulnerable time in life for Christian young people is when they first leave home to enter a new culture. For some, the experience of going to university, away from the protection of family or their home church, can be a particularly vulnerable time. Sometimes there is the added pressure of wanting to fit in with the lifestyle of those around them. For others, like Joseph, there will likely be the added pain of loneliness. The need for closeness and companionship can often lead to trying to fill that emptiness through sexual fulfilment. If you are going to university or have responsibility for those who are going, get prepared to stand!

There are other crisis times in life that can hit people hard. For some older single people, there can be a sense of impatience and a desire to short-cut God's plan. For married couples with young children, there can be issues of tiredness and maybe a temporary waning of romance and sexual drive that challenge the relationship. Similarly, for those in mid-life, the experience of an identity crisis, sometimes coupled with children leaving home, can be a point of particular vulnerability.

It is important to realise that most Bible-believing Christians don't wake up one day and plan to commit adultery or get into other forms of sexual sin. But the devil, knowing the strong, God-given desire for sexual intimacy and fulfilment, often comes to us at our most vulnerable in an attempt to seduce us from God's best for our lives. Being alert to when we are most likely to be vulnerable and taking steps to be especially vigilant will help us to say 'no' to the devil and 'yes' to God.

Why?

There are different reasons why we can be vulnerable to sexual temptation. The most obvious general fact is that as human beings we are created with sexual desires and it takes self-control to say 'no'. But there may also be specific points of vulnerability depending on our background and temperament. Sometimes, for example, we can struggle more than we should because of areas of unrepented sexual sin in previous generations or our own past lifestyle, which may be giving the devil a foothold.

Most obviously, though, we can be tempted sexually because of an attraction to another person. We must be clear that attraction is not, in itself, sin. It is what we do with those feelings in our mind and in our actions that will determine the outcome. In Joseph's case it was an issue of physical attraction. The fact that he was well built and handsome drew the unwanted attention of a married woman. More often than not the issue is reversed, with men in particular being attracted by the visual. But whether you are male or female, it is important to re-emphasise that it is not wrong to be attracted by somebody of the opposite sex. It is wrong, however, to indulge in that attraction and allow it to become a fantasy or lust.

In this whole area of physical attraction it is important that we maintain a balanced perspective. Since God made men and women beautiful and attractive, it is important that we don't succumb to a wrong religious straitjacket that causes people to cover up almost in shame. Nor is there any virtue in deliberate frumpiness or wearing clothes that make us look 20 years older than we actually are! On the other hand, we must be careful not to flaunt or flirt. To women in particular, it is important to make sure that your tops are not too low or your skirts too short. But within this overall principle of modesty, it is good to make the best of what God has given you and within the context of the marriage relationship to have fun and be sexy!

It is important, however, to realise that attraction doesn't just begin and end on a physical level. For women, there can be an even stronger pull in the areas of emotional and spiritual compatibility. As Christians we need to be alert, especially in one-on-one situations, but also in ministry teams and small group settings, that genuine unity and respect for members of the opposite sex (or same sex) doesn't open the door to lust or adultery. You need to realise that there are certain people who you will be more drawn to than others, especially if there is a combination of spiritual, emotional and physical attraction. This is, of course, not necessarily wrong. If you are single and the other person is also single and a committed Christian then it may be a 'sign' that you are supposed to get to know them better! However, we would all do well to heed the apostle Paul's exhortation to Timothy: 'Treat younger men as brothers, older women as mothers, and younger women as sisters, with absolute purity' (1 Tim. 5:1–2).

But temptation is not just with those we know, but through the very widespread, freely available and utterly destructive medium of pornography. For years this has been accessed through art, books, magazines and films, but now the situation has been greatly exacerbated by the easy availability of porn on the internet. It is vital to be aware of the dangers of pornography and, if you are aware of a weakness in this area, to be particularly vigilant.

Where?

We must be alert to the fact that in certain settings we are especially vulnerable. Having failed to seduce Joseph over a period of time, Mrs Potiphar seized the particular opportunity when 'none of the household servants was inside' (Gen. 39:11) to make one final assault. Being alone with a member of the opposite sex, in private, makes you particularly vulnerable. Years ago, I adopted a practice whereby I would not counsel a lady on her own in a private place or, for example, drive in a car on my own with a member of the opposite sex. This is just common sense. It may not be that there is even any potential problem, but it is good practice and an important safeguard.

Sadly, I am aware of too many, including Christian leaders, who have violated these basic principles. In one instance a pastor fell into adultery having gone on a mission trip on his own with a Christian lady who was not his wife! Such folly is not confined to those in leadership. A good friend of mine in Christian leadership told me of a young man who came wanting help and advice because he and his girlfriend had started sleeping together before marriage. Having heard the young man's story, my friend's advice was very straightforward: 'First, don't babysit together in the house on your own. Second, don't take your clothes off. Third, don't get into bed together!' I have sometimes heard people say that they have a boyfriend or girlfriend coming from another city to stay and that they will be sleeping on the floor, but that all will be fine. But why place yourself in such a vulnerable position and why act in a way that may give a wrong impression or unhelpful encouragement to others in a similar situation?

How?

For Joseph, the 'how' came boldly and persistently. There was nothing subtle about Mrs Potiphar:

> *'after a while his master's wife took notice of Joseph and said,*
> *"Come to bed with me!" ... she spoke to Joseph day after day'*
> (Gen. 39:7,10)

'Day after day' is often how temptation comes. Wouldn't it be wonderful if temptation only came once and, having resisted it, that was the end? But it is rarely that simple!

But not only was the temptation persistent, it was verbal: 'she spoke to Joseph'. This can be the most dangerous weapon available. In the book of

Proverbs, for example, as well as general teaching on the power of words, the writer highlights that speech was the primary tool in the hands of the adulteress:

'With persuasive words she led him astray; she seduced him with her smooth talk.' (Prov. 7:21)

Words create pictures and the woman in this passage goes to great lengths to paint a picture of the feast that awaited the naïve young man. This was the weapon that Joseph was assaulted with.

We need to be alert to not delivering or receiving words that could be potentially seductive in any way. Giving encouragement and paying compliments to others is one thing, but we must be careful of the nature of such comments. It is one thing to say to someone of the opposite sex, 'I think you are doing a great job, I really appreciate you.' It's another to stand and look into their eyes and say, 'You're looking especially gorgeous today!'

Once we realise our vulnerability, we must then steadfastly...

Refuse to compromise

This was what Joseph did. Scripture records how:

'he refused ... he refused to go bed with her or even to be with her ...
he left his cloak in her hand and ran out of the house.' (Gen. 39:8,10,12)

In other words, he made and kept on making a radical choice to stand for righteousness. He refused to compromise his integrity. He chose God's 'way out'. His stand was firm, consistent and wholehearted. In refusing to even be with her, he demonstrated the vital principle of not even giving an inch to the temptation. And in running out, he did the wise thing. Sometimes people say, when tempted, 'Well, I'm praying about it.' By all means pray, but when temptation comes on strong, pray *while* you are running! It's no use just praying if at the same time you are flicking through wrong TV channels or have access to porn sites on your computer, tablet or smartphone. No, take evasive action and get out! Change the package on your TV and get blocks on your devices so that you can't access those sites. If you don't know how, ask a good friend to do it for you. Don't just pray, 'God help me resist this temptation.' Also run, in Jesus' name!

I heard a while back about a businessman who travelled away a lot. He said the first thing he does when he goes into his hotel room is cut the plug off the television! That's pretty radical, isn't it? I don't know quite how he reconciles that with the hotel at the end of his stay, but at least he has made a decision beforehand not to allow potential loneliness or boredom snare him into giving in to temptation. Paul writes to Timothy:

> *'Run from anything that gives you evil thoughts ... but stay close to anything that makes you want to do right.'* (2 Tim. 2:22, TLB)

Let's be sensible, wise and make a decision to refuse to compromise. The next vital principle in enabling us to stand is to...

Recognise the sin

This is really important, because if you are not fully aware of the fact that all sexual activity outside of marriage is sin, and therefore destructive, then you will not have the inner resolve to say 'no'. We live in a culture where, sadly, many kinds of sexual sin and perversion are the norm. If you are not convinced from the Word of God and by the Spirit of God that sex outside marriage is wrong, then you can easily fall for the lie, 'Everyone else is doing it, so why don't you?' and you will not have the strength to resist.

It is important to realise that ancient Egypt was not unlike our culture in its morality, and Joseph didn't say 'no' because somehow immorality would have been culturally unacceptable. Nor did he resist by willpower alone, but rather through a revelation of the seriousness of the potential sin. His retort to Mrs Potiphar is particularly enlightening:

> *'My master has withheld nothing from me except you, because you are his wife. How then could I do such a wicked thing and sin against God?'* (Gen. 39:9)

This is amazing! Here is a young man, living centuries before the Law of Moses. He hasn't read the seventh commandment, 'You shall not commit adultery' (Exod. 20:14), because it hasn't been written. Yet somehow he realised that for him to have sex outside marriage and especially to sleep with another man's wife was a 'wicked thing'. First, it was a sin against the covenant of marriage, and second, it would have been a sin against his covenant with God.

Why was this such an important stand to take? The answer is because marriage is a covenant and sexual intimacy is supposed to be enjoyed only within the confines of this covenant relationship. So, if you are single, be encouraged by the example of a young man who, while not lacking in testosterone, managed to say 'no'. If you are in a relationship or even engaged, don't violate God's order by picking the fruit of sexual intimacy before having put down roots of commitment and covenant through marriage. (As an aside, oftentimes sex before marriage, even to your future spouse, can result in a dwindled passion for sex once you are actually married.) If you are married, then honour the covenant between you. Stay committed to one another through every season of your lives. If the passion and romance has dwindled, pray and believe for a revival! God really does want you to enjoy sex within marriage. As His people, we are called to demonstrate that marriage is a gift from the creator, and that sexual intimacy within the covenant is the only way.

But as much as Joseph knew that he was being tempted to dishonour the marriage relationship, I believe the main reason why he stood firm was because he recognised the potential liaison as a 'sin against God'.

Centuries later, the apostle Paul highlights the spiritual significance of walking in sexual purity:

> *'There's more to sex than mere skin on skin. Sex is as much spiritual mystery as physical fact. As written in Scripture, "The two become one." Since we want to become spiritually one with the Master, we must not pursue the kind of sex that avoids commitment and intimacy, leaving us more lonely than ever—the kind of sex that can never "become one."'* (1 Cor. 6:16–17, *The Message*)

Paul was warning against having sex with a prostitute and his comments were directed towards a church that had been established in the midst of the immoral culture of first-century Corinth. The prevailing philosophy was that sex, like eating a good meal, was purely a physical act and, provided nobody was harmed, it was quite OK to sleep around. Today, there is a similar philosophy around. But the Bible paints a different picture. Sex is not just a physical act, but is part of being united spiritually to the other person and a soul tie is actually formed.

If you are a Christian young person, I urge you to keep this great gift of sex for your future marriage partner. For those of you who were either not Christians before your marriage and sinned 'in ignorance' or were Christians and sinned in weakness and disobedience, then you need to repent before God. Ask Him to do a miracle, to break any wrong soul ties and to spiritually cleanse and restore you so that you and your spouse or future spouse can come together and enjoy great blessing, and true covenant and union.

How we conduct ourselves with regard to sexual purity is ultimately a key test in our relationship with the Lord. In that same passage in 1 Corinthians 6, Paul highlights this fact:

> *'There is a sense in which sexual sins are different from all others.*
> *In sexual sin we violate the sacredness of our own bodies, these bodies*
> *that were made for God-given and God-modeled love, for "becoming one"*

with another. Or didn't you realize that your body is a sacred place, the place of the Holy Spirit? Don't you see that you can't live however you please, squandering what God paid such a high price for?'
(vv18–19, *The Message*)

Our bodies are not our own but belong to God. They are temples of the Holy Spirit. We must honour His presence by staying free from all sexual sin.

Request God's help

Once we have recognised the sin, the good news is that we can request God's help. Remember the promise of Paul:

'God is faithful. He will not allow the temptation to be more than you can stand. When you are tempted, he will show you a way out so that you can endure.' (1 Cor. 10:13, NLT)

God doesn't just leave us alone to struggle in our flesh against temptation. No – He has a power greater than the strongest temptation to sin. We need to learn to turn to Him and draw strength to prevail, regularly praying the Lord's Prayer: 'lead us not into temptation, but deliver us from the evil one.' Praying preventative prayers is a smart way to pray. But if and when temptation does come, then we need to learn to pray simple prayers such as 'Help!'

We have no real insight as to whether Joseph specifically prayed and asked for God's help. What we do know is that 'God was with him and rescued him from all his troubles' (Acts 7:9–10). But there are abundant examples in the Bible of individuals turning to the Lord for deliverance, as well as numerous promises of His help. To take just one instance, there is the encouragement of Psalm 91:

'The LORD says, "I will rescue those who love me. I will protect those who trust in my name. When they call on me, I will answer; I will be with them in trouble. I will rescue and honor them. I will reward them with a long life and give them my salvation."' (vv14–16, NLT)

If you are under attack right now, then call on God. He will answer you and rescue you!

Refocus on Christ

What we dwell on, we tend to live in. Do you realise that the key is to win the battle of the mind? In the Garden of Eden, the devil used the power of suggestion to trap Eve, and he is still employing the same tactics today.

I'm not a great fan of Greek mythology, but I want to share with you a story from one of the myths. One of the major characters, Odysseus, was part of the company that went from Greece to invade Troy. On his journey back home to Ithaca he is called to face a number of key challenges, one of the most dangerous of which was sailing past the island of the Sirens. Many sailors had already been destroyed as they listened to the sound of the Sirens, demonic creatures who would sing a beautiful and alluring song. As the sailors drew nearer to listen, their ships would get broken up on hidden rocks and the men would be devoured by the demons.

To counteract this lethal threat, Odysseus instructed his crew to stuff their ears so that they couldn't hear the songs. They were to keep rowing forward and not look to the right or the left. He however, wanted to listen to the sounds himself, so he deliberately kept his ears open, but had the sailors strap him to the mast. As they went past the island, Odysseus was totally captivated by the sounds of the Sirens. Everything in him wanted to go and give in to the seduction. But, because he was strapped to the mast and the crew kept on rowing, they made it through.

We can try to resist temptation like Odysseus. In our hearts there is something that really wants to give in, but the fear of consequences, or the knowledge of religious upbringing, rules and regulations, keeps us strapped in and we try to resist with gritted teeth. This trying to resist sin through the power of the flesh with the constraints of the Law is a wearying and ultimately self-defeating process.

There is, however, a better way! Jason, another mythological character, adopted a totally different approach. His ship's crew were told to keep their ears open and he would not be strapped to the mast. As they passed by the Sirens, he instructed a brilliant musician, Orpheus, to play his most beautiful melody. As Jason and his crew were captivated by this more wonderful sound, the Sirens lost their power over them and the ship passed safely by.

We have two choices as to how to resist temptation. Either we can battle on through willpower alone, inwardly longing to give in, or we can allow our lives to be transformed by the more beautiful song of knowing the amazing love and grace of God in Christ. I want my 'no' to sin to arise from a cry of 'yes' to the Son of God. I want to love the things that God loves and hate what He hates not simply because that is what I'm supposed to do, but because that is what I long to do.

The greatest antidote to sin is God's love filling every part of us so that we're not captivated by another seductive song. Yes, we need to choose to say 'no'. Yes, we need to exercise discipline in our lives. Yes, we need to be wise and keep out of compromising situations. But we are not to walk through life with our ears stuffed or our eyes covered over, saying through gritted teeth, 'I must not sin, I must not sin.' Instead, we are to be captivated by a better sound. We must be filled with the love of God, over and over again. This comes first as we realise, time and again, how radical His grace and acceptance is in Christ. Then, day by day, morning by morning, we come to His throne of grace (Heb. 4:16), drawing near to spend time with Him, receiving from His Word and His Spirit, enjoying intimate fellowship with Him, and hearing Him say, 'I love you!'

Reveal your struggle

No matter how strong your love for Christ, your prayer life, or your self-discipline, there are times when you will need to share your inner battles with other mature, Christian friends or leaders. The good news is that, unlike Joseph, who was clearly isolated in his struggle, you don't need to deal with temptation alone, but can be part of a spiritual family, the Church. As you bring areas of weakness and temptation to the light, sin loses its power over you. The writer of Ecclesiastes highlights the importance of companionship in life:

> *'Two people are better off than one, for they can help each other succeed. If one person falls, the other can reach out and help. But someone who falls alone is in real trouble.'* (4:9–10, NLT)

Jesus Himself modelled this principle, most notably at Gethsemane. Facing His greatest test, nearly overwhelmed with what was to come, He not only prayed to His Father, but shared His inner struggles with His three closest friends (not that they were much help to Him, since they kept falling asleep, but that is another matter!). My question to you is: do you have either one, two or maybe three people who you know well enough and trust spiritually who you can share your inner struggles with when you feel overwhelmed? To quote Rick Warren in his book *The Purpose Driven Life*:

> *'Don't repress it; confess it! Don't conceal it; reveal it … You are only as sick as your secrets. So take off your mask, stop pretending you're perfect, and walk into freedom.'*[3]

Revealing your struggle may be the last thing you feel you want to do. Sharing troubling thoughts with another may seem frightening, but providing you choose your friends carefully, it is the best thing you can do. If you have sinned, catch it early, before it gets a greater hold. Repent before God, but also ask others to stand with you:

> *'Confess your sins to each other and pray for each other so that you may be healed. The earnest prayer of a righteous person has great power and produces wonderful results.'* (James 5:16, NLT)

Run from sin, run to God and run for help in Jesus' name! Then you will be in a position to consistently...

Resist the devil

In the Joseph narrative there is no mention of the devil, rather an emphasis on a sovereign God and sinful people. But earlier in Genesis, Satan, represented by the serpent, is seen as the active power behind temptation (Gen. 3). Later, in the New Testament with the coming of Jesus, the work of Satan is more fully exposed. While not giving the devil undue attention, we are exhorted not to be ignorant of his devices either (2 Cor. 2:11). Sexual sin is not just a physical act, but a spiritual decision that opens the door to the devil and to unclean spirits. It is far better never to open the door in the first place:

> *'Submit yourselves, then, to God. Resist the devil, and he will flee from you.'* (James 4:7)

First, we have to submit ourselves to God, which gives us the authority to stand firm in the Lord and in His mighty power, and then put on the whole armour of God. The final piece of armour (and the only one with any offensive capabilities) is the 'sword of the Spirit, which is the word of God' (Eph. 6:17). This 'word' in the Greek is the *rhema* – the spoken word empowered by the Spirit, which allied with praying in the Spirit (Eph. 6:18) brings complete defeat for the devil. It was the weapon that Jesus used in the wilderness (Matt. 4) and is vital for us to employ too. In this epic battle, Jesus quoted three times from the book of Deuteronomy to defeat the devil's temptations. The clear implication is that somehow Jesus must have learnt these verses and digested them ready for later use. We, too, must prepare ourselves for battle not just by hearing, reading or studying God's Word (all of which are vital), but we must go a step further and memorise and then meditate on specific portions of Scripture, ready to be used under the Spirit's direction in the heat of the battle. We would do well to heed the encouragement of the psalmist:

> *'How can a young person stay on the path of purity? By living according to your word ... I have hidden your word in my heart that I might not sin against you.'* (Psa. 119:9,11)

Rather than simply trying to resist the devil in your mind, do things the Jesus way: speak God's Word out loud and watch the enemy flee. When you have successfully resisted the devil there is a promise that ultimately you will...

Receive your reward

In Joseph's case, his reward was certainly not instantaneous. In fact, his righteous stand resulted in years in prison! But ultimately, in terms of God's destiny for his life, his right choice was vital and his triumph assured. The incredible promotion, prosperity and longevity that he later enjoyed are testimony to God's great vindication and reward. For you, too, you may have had to or will have to make a stand for integrity and initially it may not be well-received and in the short run look like it is costing you dearly. But I want to encourage you: God, the eternal judge, doesn't miss a thing. He is the great rewarder of those who faithfully walk in His ways. Be encouraged:

> *'God blesses those who patiently endure testing and temptation. Afterward they will receive the crown of life that God has promised to those who love him.'* (James 1:12, NLT)

Joseph passed this big test, God rewarded him and he ended up living the dream. God can and will do the same for you, too. In this life, and certainly in the next, the great rewards are on their way!

CHAPTER 5

PROSPERING IN TOUGH TIMES

The third test Joseph faced and subsequently passed was the fruitfulness test. While learning to forgive those who had offended him and be *faithful* in overcoming sexual temptation, he also became *fruitful* and prospered even in the toughest of times. First as a slave and then as a prisoner, he enjoyed remarkable blessing and promotion. Rather than waiting for his 'big break' and the obvious fulfilment of his dreams, he got on, worked hard and enjoyed success, even when outwardly the situation looked desperate. Instead of sitting around and feeling sorry for himself, he prospered even in the midst of great adversity. He persevered and eventually prevailed.

One of the greatest examples of perseverance is Abraham Lincoln. Born into poverty, Lincoln was faced with adversity throughout his life. He lost eight elections, failed twice in business and suffered a nervous breakdown. He could have quit many times – but he didn't and because he didn't quit, he became one of the greatest presidents in the history of the United States of America.

Like Joseph and Abraham Lincoln, we often have to persevere through tough times before we can start living the dream. During this waiting season, God is at work, shaping and refining our character. But instead of simply waiting and hoping for better days, God wants to teach us to walk with Him and enjoy His blessing on our lives, even when the circumstances seem difficult and the opportunities limited. Then, and only then, will we be ready for greater blessing and responsibility, and able to walk in the fullness of what the Lord has in store for us.

We need to realise that in whatever sphere of life – be it in the marketplace or church-based ministry – there is no such thing as an overnight success. If we are promoted too quickly without the proper foundations having been laid in our lives, we will probably not be ready to handle what lies ahead. We will be like the Leaning Tower of Pisa, always lopsided due to weak and insufficient foundations. Rather than feeling self-pity or waiting aimlessly for a lottery-winning moment, we must realise that God has a key purpose for 'delays'. If you feel you are working and ministering in a situation where there is not much evidence of outward breakthrough or public profile, then realise that God is the God of the hidden season too.

As we have seen in Chapter 2, Joseph's apprenticeship was particularly tough, lasting a total of 13 years. His first assignment was as a slave, working for an Egyptian captain of the guard, hundreds of miles from home in a foreign country and culture with no rights or freedom (Gen. 39:1–6). His second was in an Egyptian prison (39:20–23). Although a strategic place in which the king's prisoners were held, and probably not the worst jail he could have ended up in, it was certainly no five star hotel! Both situations were very tough and the 'training' would have been particularly arduous. Yet, in both places Joseph prospered in a remarkable way. This was due to two main factors: the *presence* of God and the *favour* of God. The former tells us something about Joseph's *vertical* relationship with the Lord and the latter is the result of it, manifested in his *horizontal* relationships with others.

Key 1: the presence of God

The primary reason Joseph prospered in tough times was the presence of God. The text highlights this vital fact by repeating the same truth three times in the one chapter:

> 'The LORD was with Joseph ... the LORD was with him ... the LORD was with him' (Gen. 39:2,3,21)

Later, in the book of Acts, Stephen similarly emphasises that in spite of Joseph's troubles, 'God was with him' (Acts 7:9).

What is not made clear in either account is how or in what way God was with him. But this repeated emphasis on God's presence is Scripture's way of highlighting to us that it was because of God's sovereign hand upon him that Joseph prospered. This is an amazing thought for us, too. When the presence of Almighty God, the creator and ruler of the universe is with us, we can prosper in every season of our lives. When His hand is upon us, all things are possible!

So what does it mean to have God with us? On one level we can say that because God is omnipresent He is always with us. But the emphasis here is that God was with Joseph, and wants to be with us, in a more *personal* way. He was with Joseph as He was with his forefathers in the earlier chapters of Genesis – as a covenant-keeping God, blessing them and making them a blessing (Gen. 12:2–3). But the way that God revealed Himself to Joseph was different. There are no indications, for example, that He appeared in a theophany as He did to Abraham and Jacob. Yet the presence of God was sufficiently evident in Joseph's life to receive prominent attention in both the Genesis account and in the later Acts summary. If experiencing God's presence was a key to Joseph prospering in adversity, then it is similarly important for us today. If that is so, then we need to briefly examine how we can know His presence with us in an ever-increasing way...

By receiving His presence as a gift

First, we must make clear that the presence of God is not something deserved or earned, but rather is a gift to be received. While Jesus was on the earth, people had the privilege of experiencing the presence of God through His own Son. But dramatic and intense as this undoubtedly was, there is no suggestion that the early disciples (let alone the Old Testament patriarchs or prophets before them) somehow had a better opportunity to experience the presence of God than we do now. In fact, Jesus makes it quite clear that the opposite is true. In John 14–16 He prepared His disciples for His death, resurrection and ascension to the Father and made the following remarkable promise:

> *'I will ask the Father, and he will give you another advocate to*
> *help you and be with you for ever – the Spirit of truth ... you know*
> *him, for he lives with you and will be in you. I will not leave you as*
> *orphans; I will come to you.'* (John 14:16–18)

This is a wonderful truth! Jesus is promising His disciples that when He goes to the Father they will not be left alone. Instead, through another 'helper', just like Him, Jesus will still be present with them. This Spirit of truth will be all that Jesus was to them. Except now, things will be even better. With Jesus physically present, they only knew the Spirit 'with them'. With Jesus absent, they will now have the Spirit permanently 'in them'. This was better by far. So much so that Jesus could say:

> *'But very truly I tell you, it is for your good that I am going away. Unless I go away, the Advocate will not come to you; but if go, I will send him to you.'* (John 16:7)

This is a central truth that many Christians still fail to grasp. It is better to have Jesus in heaven and the Spirit on earth, because it means that now God is in us *and* with us 24/7, for the rest of our days on earth, before we see him 'face to face' on the final day. This is certainly better than the experience of Joseph and the faithful believers who lived under the old covenant. We now have the Holy Spirit, leading and guiding and empowering us throughout every situation and circumstance of our lives.

If Joseph could prevail in his trials because God was with him, how much more can we prevail knowing that we have the Lord both with us and in us, through the permanent indwelling of the Holy Spirit? No wonder that the apostle Paul, writing about the ministry of the Holy Spirit in the wonderful chapter 8 of Romans, was able to triumphantly conclude that neither trouble nor hardship, nor persecution, nor famine, nor nakedness, nor danger, nor sword, nor any other tough or challenging circumstance in life could separate believers from the love of Christ. Rather:

> *'in all these things we are more than conquerors through him who loved us. For I am convinced that neither death nor life, neither angels nor demons, neither the present nor the future, nor any powers,*

neither height nor depth, nor anything else in all creation, will be able to separate us from the love of God that is in Christ Jesus our Lord.'
(Rom. 8:37–39)

The abiding, comforting, triumphal presence of God is available to all believers everywhere in every situation!

But it is one thing to know 'by faith' that God has graciously poured out His Spirit in and upon us, and another to actively appropriate His presence in our daily lives and to cultivate this so that we experience the reality of it in every situation. In order to do so, it is not enough just to have received the Spirit by grace through faith, we need to cultivate His manifest presence in our lives. We do this by...

Developing an intimate relationship with God

While it is clear that we don't earn the presence of God, we can position ourselves, through faith and obedience, to receive more of His blessing on our lives. This tension between God's grace and our faith-filled obedient response to His grace runs right through the Scriptures. Already, in the foundational chapters of Genesis 1–11, the narrator has presented a clear message that disobedience results in being cast out from the presence and blessing of God – whether in the case of Adam and Eve, Cain, the godless generation before the Flood, Ham or the men at Babel. In the same way, favour and blessing is bestowed on those who walk in obedience before God, be it Abel, Enoch, Noah, Shem or Abraham. Similarly, the fact that God was 'with' Joseph in an evident way, is implicitly attributed to his faithful life.

Significantly, Joseph is later included among the 'heroes' of Hebrews 11 who were all commended for their faith-filled obedience, seen as essential for pleasing God. How are we to appropriate this faith? According to the apostle Paul:

'faith comes by hearing, and hearing by the word of God.'
(Rom. 10:17, NKJV)

If faith-filled obedience is the key to walking in the manifest grace and blessing of God, and faith comes from hearing the Word of God, then a vital key is to learn to *listen to God's voice.*

The writer of Genesis is largely silent about how Joseph communed with God, other than telling us that God spoke to him through dreams and the interpretation of dreams (see the next chapter), but throughout the Bible, from Abraham to Moses to David to Jesus and to Paul, we see that great men of God consistently maintained a dynamic, personal relationship with the Lord. Their private devotional life was a major key to their success in public ministry and in fulfilling their God-appointed destiny.

I believe one of the most important lessons we can learn, especially in a season of preparation, is the need to develop our personal relationship with God. Very early on in my Christian life, I discovered the benefit of developing a loving and consistent, two-way relationship with the Lord. Whatever season you are in right now, I want to encourage you to put down deep roots in the soil of God's love. You must learn to love the Lord of the work before being fully released into the work of the Lord! If you can do this in adversity and obscurity, then you won't be ruined by prosperity and prominence. Over the years, I have experienced and taught the importance of finding a *time,* a *place* and a *way* to meet with God. I would like to share briefly on all three of these...

1. Time

There is no substitute for spending quality time with God. We see this in the life of Jesus, where even He, the Son of God, clearly needed to prioritise quality time with His Father (Mark 1:35; Luke 6:12). For me, this has always worked best first thing in the morning, but for you the best time of the day is when you are at your best!

2. Place

Similarly, the place or places where we meet with God are often equally important. Jesus tended to go out into solitary places or up mountains to pray (Mark 1:35,45), and the implication is that He also had a favourite place, the Mount of Olives, where He most liked to pray. On the edge of the Fenlands where I live there are certainly no mountains, but over the years I too have found certain places, especially outdoors, that have worked well.

3. Way

Once we have established a daily discipline of regular times and places, we must find practical ways of meeting with the Lord. There are many, but two are primary: hearing God through His Word and speaking to Him through prayer.

Daily Bible reading and journaling

Having experimented over the years, I am convinced that as much as possible we need to learn to *listen* to the Lord before *speaking* to Him. Interestingly, before Jesus teaches the principles of prayer in Luke 11, Luke records the incident of Mary and Martha in Luke 10:38–42. Here Mary is commended because she is sitting at Jesus' feet, listening to His words. If our relationship with the Lord is to be two-way, then it is important for us to realise that what He has to say to us is more important that whatever we have to say to Him!

We must also realise that the primary and best way in which God speaks to us is through His written Word by His Holy Spirit (though, of course, not the only way that God speaks, as we have seen from Chapter 1 and we shall see in Chapter 6). The experience of Christians throughout the generations has shown that a key to consistently hearing from God is by systematically reading the Bible on a daily basis, expecting Him to speak. Then, as the Lord prompts, it is good to write down and act upon what He is saying.

A book that I have found particularly helpful in this regard has been Wayne Cordeiro's *The Divine Mentor*. Wayne emphasises the importance of listening to God through the Scriptures, and introduces a simple and practical way to do this through the acronym SOAP. The 'S' stands for Scripture. Having read a few chapters of the Bible (through a regular plan), the goal is to ask the Holy Spirit to highlight one verse or short passage for that day and then write it down. The 'O' stands for Observation – an encouragement to objectively reflect on and write down the meaning of the text and its context. This then leads on to 'A', the Application section, where we write down what the Lord has spoken *specifically* into our life and circumstances. The exercise concludes with 'P' as we Pray back to God in relation to what He has spoken.

It amazes me how often I sense the Lord speaking specifically to me through this simple pattern of consistent Bible reading and journaling. With this listening foundation in place, we can move on to responding to God in prayer.

Prayer

In 1 Corinthians 14:15, Paul highlights the dual aspect of prayer:

'I will pray with my spirit, but I will also pray with my understanding; I will sing with my spirit, but I will also sing with my understanding.'

First, Paul mentions praying 'with my spirit'. In context, this is clearly more than simply praying in one's own language as the Spirit leads (as vital as that is), but refers to praying 'in other tongues'. Paul says that first he prays or sings in the Spirit or in tongues. This, I believe is a vital and sadly often misunderstood or much neglected way of connecting with the Lord and enjoying His presence in our lives.

For me personally, I had been a Christian for about eighteen months and was enjoying a measure of the presence of God in my life. But my spiritual walk was transformed when I was prayed over and received an empowering from the Holy Spirit and was released into speaking in other tongues. This experience described by some as the 'infilling of the Spirit' and by others as the 'baptism in the Spirit', has sadly been the cause of much confusion, division and dissension. My purpose in sharing my testimony is not to add to this, but simply to encourage those who have not received this experience that it is very beneficial, and for those who can speak in tongues to actually speak in tongues regularly. For years I have seen the amazing benefit of praying in tongues: being able to express my praise to God beyond my own vocabulary (Acts 10:46); being able to pray for situations beyond my understanding (Rom. 8:26–27); and being personally strengthened and edified by the Holy Spirit as I pray (1 Cor. 14:2,4; Jude 20).

But Paul emphasises the importance of praying with our minds or 'understanding' too. There are many different ways to pray and Paul himself left us some great model prayers to use (Eph. 1; 3; Col. 1). I discovered a real key when, as a young Christian, I heard a series of teachings on how to pray through the Lord's Prayer. Up until that point, while I had a real desire to pray, I found myself frustrated and often discouraged by the way my mind wandered. While I still have to discipline my mind to stay on track, I have found over the years that the framework of the Lord's Prayer helps me stay focused.

I start by honouring God, who is my Father, and begin to enter His presence. As I worship His name, so my revelation of Him and His love begins to increase. As I declare His kingdom over my own life, family and ministry, I experience an ordering and covering of my world. As I pray daily and specifically for personal and ministry financial needs, I see His provision on a regular basis. As I confess my sins to Him and release others, so I continue to walk in His freedom and peace. As I humble myself to walk in His ways and claim His protection, I see triumph over temptation and victory over the evil one. And as I declare God's kingdom, power and glory, so I go out into my day with a sense of joy and praise. Put simply, praying the Lord's Prayer really works!

There are, of course, many and varied ways to develop our relationship with the Lord: worshipping to music, contemplating the Lord's magnificence in creation, fasting, and participating wholeheartedly and regularly in corporate gatherings to mention but a few. If you are in a 'hidden' testing season in your life, maximise the opportunity to develop a deep and abiding confidence in the presence of God. As you develop your vertical relationship with Him, you can be assured that in His sovereign timing and way, you will experience breakthrough and blessing, and like Joseph, you will enjoy...

Key 2: the favour of God

In Joseph's season of preparation, the link between the presence of God and the favour of God was abundantly clear:

> *'The Lord was with Joseph so that he prospered ... the Lord was with*
> *him and ... gave him success in everything he did'* (Gen. 39:2–3)

To be successful in everything you do is to live in ultimate fruitfulness. So evident was the favour of the Lord on Joseph that Potiphar, his master, promoted him:

> *'Joseph found favour in [Potiphar's] eyes and became his attendant.*
> *Potiphar put him in charge of his household, and he entrusted to his*
> *care everything he owned. From the time he put him in charge of his*
> *household and of all that he owned, the Lord blessed the household*
> *and of the Egyptian because of Joseph. The blessing of the Lord*
> *was on everything Potiphar had, both in the house and in the field.*
> *So Potiphar left everything he had in Joseph's care'* (Gen. 39:4–6)

This is a truly remarkable transformation. From being a slave, Joseph ended up running the whole household! The presence and blessing of God in his life was so evident that his Egyptian master gave him almost total responsibility for all his affairs.

A similar picture is painted of Joseph in prison:

> *'But while Joseph was there in the prison, the Lord was with him;*
> *he showed him kindness and granted him favour in the eyes of the*
> *prison warder. So the warder put Joseph in charge of all those held in*

*the prison, and he was made responsible for all that was done there.
The warder paid no attention to anything under Joseph's care, because
the LORD was with Joseph and gave him success in whatever he did.'*
(Gen. 39:20–23)

Here, again, the presence and favour of God led to supernatural success, causing favour with man and the assignment of greater responsibility. This is extremely encouraging! I believe there is no limit to what the Lord can do in and through His covenant people. God's favour can open doors of opportunity that are truly astonishing. When the favour of God is with you, then the world will sit up and take notice, and this favour, by definition, is a gift.

But while the passage very clearly attributes the cause and credit for Joseph's success to God, there must have been something about the way that Joseph himself appropriated and walked in that blessing that attracted the attention of a hard-nosed Egyptian captain of the guard and a prison warder. Similarly, if we are to be entrusted with the blessing of God, we must be ready to allow this favour to manifest in such a way that others sit up and take notice. The first thing we must do is...

Be ready to prosper in the present

This may sound obvious, but it is a vital point to make. The tendency we can sometimes have, especially if we have a dream for greater purpose and blessing in our lives, is to wait for the 'big break' before we start prospering. But Joseph didn't do that. He prospered where he was. He didn't just wait for a better future, he started excelling in the present. This is so important. Otherwise, in the name of wanting to live the dream, we can get into an escapist mentality, always waiting, always 'on the brink' of something great but never achieving it. It is crucial, while waiting in faith for the fulfilment of God's purposes, that we don't spend our whole time focusing on tomorrow, but rather get on with living each day in the presence and favour of God. Jesus Himself was very clear on this: 'Therefore do not worry about tomorrow, for tomorrow will worry about itself. Each day has enough trouble of its own' (Matt. 6:34).

This is not a word against future dreams or planning, but it clearly highlights that we need to learn to live day by day, trusting in a Father who can take care of tomorrow. If we are to prosper in the present, then the vast majority of us also need to learn to...

Honour our earthly boss

Joseph 'lived in the house of his Egyptian master', a man called Potiphar. Potiphar was the captain of the guard and background studies suggest he was probably an extremely ruthless man. He was Joseph's first boss. His second was the prison warder. The attitude of many today is, 'I'll honour my boss if he or she is nice to me, encourages me and is fair in every aspect of managing me'! But the New Testament makes clear that we are not given the luxury of honouring only those employers who are good. In writing to slaves, Paul exhorts:

> *'obey your earthly masters in everything; and do it, not only when their eye is on you and to [win] their favour, but with sincerity of heart and reverence for the Lord.'* (Col. 3:22)

This doesn't mean that we are to obey to the point of sinning against God, but the very clear teaching here is that we are to look to a higher authority, the Lord Himself:

> *'Whatever you do, work at it with all your heart, as working for the Lord, not for human masters, since you know that you will receive an inheritance from the Lord as a reward. It is the Lord Christ you are serving.'* (Col. 3:23–24)

Why don't you, right now where you are, make the following decision: 'I'm going to be trustworthy in all that I do. Whatever I do, in the home or at work, I'm doing it for You, Lord. You are my ultimate boss.' This will lead to you being the best employee you can possibly be, working hard, being punctual and keeping a good attitude, even when it is hard going. It really isn't a question of whether you like your current employer or not, but rather about serving them faithfully as a way of honouring the Lord. Those who run their own business or are self-employed can also apply this principle, honouring God by conducting their business with integrity and faithfulness. Interestingly, Joseph always worked for an earthly boss: first Potiphar, then the prison warder and then Pharaoh. None of them worshipped Yahweh and all of them, in their own way, would have been hard taskmasters. Yet, Joseph ended up being promoted to second-in-command to all three.

What an impact on the world we would see if every Christian employee learned the lesson of Joseph and lived an exemplary life of hard work, effectiveness and integrity in the workplace. I believe that people would start taking more notice of the glorious gospel of Jesus. Most people around us are less interested in what we do on a Sunday morning than how we live our lives on a Monday morning. When they start seeing the favour of God working in and through us, they will be more likely to ask 'Why?'

In a key passage, the apostle Peter unpacks the importance of our witness in the world:

> 'Live such good lives among the pagans that, though they accuse you of doing wrong, they may see your good deeds and glorify God on the day he visits us. Submit yourselves for the Lord's sake to every human authority: whether to the emperor, as the supreme authority, or to governors, who are sent by him to punish those who do wrong and to commend those who do right. For it is God's will that by doing good you should silence the ignorant talk of foolish people. Live as free people, but do not use your freedom as a cover-up for evil; live as God's slaves. Show proper respect to everyone, love the family of believers, fear God, honour the emperor. Slaves, in reverent fear of God submit yourselves to your masters, not only to those who are good and considerate, but also to those who are harsh.' (1 Pet. 2:12–18)

Peter is contending for an integrated lifestyle that affects every area of human relationships and includes honouring authorities, be they in government or at work. This is the opposite of the compartmentalised attitude that many Christians carry around, living one way 'in church' and another 'at work'. Joseph is a great example to us of a man of God walking in the presence and favour of God, yet displaying such an attitude that his pagan bosses want to keep promoting him! As the people of God, let us live as if God is our boss and honour those we are working for.

In order to be most effective in the workplace and thereby prosper in all circumstances, we also need to...

Be faithful in using the gifts that God has given us

This will be the main theme of the next chapter and a key to Joseph's promotion before Pharaoh. But here we simply need to highlight the fact that God had clearly given Joseph a gift of leadership and administration, and he exercised this during this tough preparation season. What caused Potiphar and the prison warder to recognise the presence and favour of God on him was not a heavenly glow around him, but the fact that he got the job done exceedingly well! As a result, he was quickly promoted despite being a foreign slave and prisoner.

Faithfully using his God-given abilities was not only vital in Joseph prospering where he was, but was also essential preparation for where he was heading. The lessons that he learned from running Potiphar's household and the prison, stood him in great stead for later running the country. This is so important for us, too. If we are ever to be ready to live the dream that God has for us, we must get ready and be trained for what lies ahead. Can I encourage you then: don't despise the day of small things. If, right now, you feel you are working or ministering in an obscure and even very frustrating environment, God has a purpose for you there. If you will be faithful in learning to use and hone the gifts God has given you in this season, then you are far more likely not only to prosper where you are right now, but to be ready for the greater promotion that lies ahead.

Walk with God on a daily basis, enjoy the presence of His Spirit, expect His favour to manifest where you are, right now, and watch what He will do!

CHAPTER 6

YOUR GIFTS WILL
MAKE A WAY

After preparation comes promotion! Thirteen of the best years of Joseph's life, seemingly wasted in slavery and prison, were in fact preparation for a spectacular promotion to the second highest position in the most powerful empire in the world. When God knew that Joseph was ready, He promoted him *through the gifts He had given him*. Centuries later, Stephen highlighted the sovereign hand of God who had rescued Joseph from all his troubles and noted how:

> *'God gave him favour before Pharaoh, king of Egypt. God also gave Joseph unusual wisdom, so that Pharaoh appointed him governor over all of Egypt and put him in charge of the palace.'* (Acts 7:10, NLT)

God is clearly presented as the source of Joseph's elevation, giving him favour with Pharaoh. The way the Lord promoted Joseph was by giving him 'unusual wisdom'. In other words, it was Joseph's God-given gift that made a way for him.

God wants to make a way for you too, by working in and through you, not in spite of you. However, He doesn't just want to raise you up as an individual 'Joseph', but rather to place you in connection with a 'Joseph company': a group of differently gifted but wonderfully united men and women in a local church, who together can make a harmonious sound that will cause the world to stop and wonder. The first thing to grasp is that...

You have received gifts from God

The consistent message of the New Testament is that every believer has been given certain gifts. In Romans 12:6, for example, Paul writes: 'In his grace, God has given us different gifts for doing certain things well' (NLT). There then follows a list of seven different 'gifts': prophecy, serving, teaching, encouraging, giving, leadership/administration and mercy. Elsewhere, notably in Ephesians 4:11 and 1 Corinthians 12, there are other 'gift' lists. Without going into the details of possible categorisation of these various lists, the main point is clear: God gives gifts to every one of His children!

The gift that made a way for Joseph was clearly a prophetic gift. At 17 years old, he received his double dream. Years later, his gift seems to have developed so that he could interpret the dreams of others: first of Pharaoh's servants and then of Pharaoh himself. It was this remarkably accurate gift of dream interpretation that the Lord used to orchestrate Joseph's elevation.

The link between dreams and prophecy is clear throughout Scripture. For example, when the Lord rebuked Aaron and Miriam for criticising Moses, He defended His servant with whom He spoke 'face to face' and then referred to the ministry of prophecy:

'When there is a prophet among you, I, the Lord, *reveal myself to them in visions,* I speak to them in dreams.' (Num. 12:6, emphasis mine)

Similarly, on the day of Pentecost, Peter sought to explain the outpouring of the Spirit on all the gathered believers by quoting from the prophet Joel:

'In the last days, God says, I will pour out my Spirit on all people. Your sons and daughters will prophesy, your young men will see visions, your old men will dream dreams. *Even on my servants, both men and women, I will pour out my Spirit in those days, and they* will prophesy.' (Acts 2:17–18, emphases mine)

While we are all encouraged to prophesy, we are clearly not all called to be prophets. According to the apostle Peter, some have a 'speaking' gift and others have a 'serving' gift (1 Peter 4:11). But the important thing to grasp is that no matter who you are or where you come from, *you have received gifts from God.* Once you realise this...

You must faithfully use the gifts you have received

This point is brought out very forcefully in the text in 1 Peter 4:

> *'Each of you should use whatever gift you have received to serve others, as faithful stewards of God's grace in its various forms.'* (v10)

A similar exhortation is made in Romans 12:

> *'So if God has given you the ability to prophesy, speak out with as much faith as God has given you. If your gift is serving others, serve them well. If you are a teacher, teach well. If your gift is to encourage others, be encouraging. If it is giving, give generously. If God has given you leadership ability, take the responsibility seriously. And if you have a gift for showing kindness to others, do it gladly.'* (vv6–8, NLT)

Significantly, both passages emphasise the importance of faithfully using gifts in the context of serving others in and through the local church. I know that I am biased, but I think that KingsGate Community Church is filled with some of the most wonderful, servant-hearted, faithful and gifted people anywhere in the body of Christ! Together they are making an impact. A while ago, we received the following email:

Dear KingsGate,

Firstly, I want to thank you so much for your welcome last Sunday when my wife, Caroline, and I came to your 11.30am service. The moment we entered the outer gates we felt the warmth of your fellowship from the car park attendants and had been greeted three times before we even reached the door! We have known about you as a church for many years and have been looking forward to an opportunity to come and visit you. Our experience was everything we expected and more. Can we ask you particularly to thank Norman, who met us at the door and prayed for the healing of my back injury after the service (I am now fully mobile again) and Ronna, who chatted with us afterwards and then sent us a lovely card later this week. Someone in the congregation also prayed with Caroline for our future as we are seeking God's guidance for potential full-time church work (she can't remember his name, but apparently he usually plays the guitar).

Different members working together in unity and exercising their different gifts really does make a difference!

How are we to faithfully use the gifts of God? Once again, Joseph provides a wonderful example. From his life we can see a number of principles, the first of which is...

Always be ready to use your gifts

Joseph demonstrated a commendable readiness to exercise his gift of dream interpretation, particularly since it was his own dreams (or at least the communication of those dreams) that had got him into trouble in the first place. Here he was, ten years later, still firmly embedded in an Egyptian prison and the fulfilment of those dreams probably seemed a long way off, if not impossible. He may well have been tempted to doubt whether his original dreams were authentic or God-given, and may have asked himself, 'Did God really speak to me?' So the fact that he immediately responded to the opportunity to interpret the dreams of the king's servants is in itself remarkable. He clearly didn't despise the prophetic gift he had been given. Neither did he hold back through fear of the consequences of using his gift again.

This is important because we can sometimes become discouraged and doubt our God-given gifts and back off from using them. Especially early in ministry, when I first started preaching, I would often get hit with a serious case of 'post-preaching blues'. I would find myself getting assaulted with thoughts of how I had 'missed it' and that maybe I hadn't been called to preach after all. Over the years, I have learned to deal more quickly with such negative thoughts and feelings. But having talked with others, whether in preaching or leading, the feelings of doubt and failure can afflict even the most confident of types. If you are battling in this area, can I encourage you to resist negative thinking and keep believing that God has gifted and called you.

Not only can our gifts be affected by discouragement, they can also become dormant through lack of use. In the area of personal evangelism, for example, I have been struck by how much my attitude of expectancy and readiness to be used by the Lord affects how much I experience His power at work. I can go days, even weeks, without speaking to anyone about the Lord if I choose not to. But when I position myself in faith and look for opportunities, I can have God-inspired conversations almost every time I meet someone! In this respect, Peter's exhortation is particularly helpful:

'Always be prepared to give an answer to everyone who asks you to give the reason for the hope that you have. But do this with gentleness and respect' (1 Pet. 3:15)

This attitude of readiness and expectancy applies no matter what the area of ministry or gifting. We would do well to obey the exhortation of Paul to Timothy:

'I remind you to fan into flame the gift of God, which is in you through the laying on of my hands. For the Spirit God gave us does not make us timid, but gives us power, love and of self-discipline.' (2 Tim. 1:6–7)

Like Timothy, we have received gifts from God, but we have to fan them into flame, keep them stirred up and not allow fear to stop us from stepping out. Like Joseph, we mustn't allow the bad experiences of using our gifts in the past stop us stepping out again in the present and the future. Not only must we always be ready to exercise our God-given gifts, but we must...

Exercise the gifts with compassion

This will help keep our motives right. It was Joseph's compassion for his fellow prisoners that helped him walk through the door that God opened. The king's cupbearer and baker had woken up clearly troubled by their dreams, with no one to interpret for them:

> *'When Joseph came to them the next morning, he saw that they were dejected. So he asked Pharaoh's officials who were in custody with him in his master's house, "Why are your faces so sad today?" "We both had dreams," they answered, "but there is no one to interpret them."'*
> (Gen. 40:6–8)

Joseph's concern and immediate willingness to interpret their dreams showed that he had a servant attitude, sensitive to the needs of those around him and willing to help them in whatever way he could.

This is a great example for us to follow. The gifts of God only really work to their maximum effectiveness when our motivation is the love of God flowing through us to serve others. Paul's major teaching on spiritual gifts in 1 Corinthians 12 and 14, deliberately sandwiches his classic exhortation on love in chapter 13. The link between the two is succinctly summarised in 1 Corinthians 14:1:

> *'Follow the way of love and eagerly desire gifts of the Spirit, especially prophecy.'*

This was a lesson that was forcefully brought home to me as a young Christian. I remember going up to a more mature man of God and asking him to pray for me so that I might operate in the gifts of healing and miracles. His response came as a surprise: 'Why do you want those gifts?' In effect, he was rightly addressing the issue of my motivation and then proceeded to highlight that God has three main purposes for miracle ministry: to glorify His name, to expand His kingdom and to be moved with compassion to meet the needs of people.

It is important that we not only minister out of compassion, but also that we...

Acknowledge God as the source of the gifts

While Joseph was clearly willing and ready to serve others, he was also keen to honour God as his source. His response to the dreams of the baker and cupbearer demonstrated this God-ward and man-ward approach:

> 'Do not interpretations belong to God? Tell me your dreams.'
> (Gen. 40:8)

This is very different from the boastful, impulsive 17-year-old dreamer from before. Then his focus was on his own elevation above the rest of his family, without any mention of God whatsoever. Now in his late twenties, having been refined in the fire, he dared not act without first affirming that 'interpretations belong to God'. We can learn much from his example, always being careful to acknowledge God as the giver of the gifts, and ensuring that we exercise those gifts in a way that doesn't draw attention to ourselves but rather to God as our source.

This desire to honour God was apparent when, two years later, Joseph appeared before Pharaoh. Here was this Hebrew slave and prisoner, summoned to help the most powerful ruler of his day:

> 'Pharaoh said to Joseph, "I had a dream, and no one can interpret it. But I have heard it said of you that when you hear a dream you can interpret it."' (Gen. 41:15)

After 13 years of rejection, isolation and non-recognition, this was a great opportunity for Joseph's ego to get massaged! But his response was striking:

> '"I cannot do it," Joseph replied to Pharaoh, "but God will give Pharaoh the answer he desires."' (Gen. 41:16)

The sense of progression from the earlier prison scene is subtle but significant. There, he did acknowledge God as the source, but his first words were, 'Tell me your dreams.' Here, he seems so humbled before God that his first words to this great ruler who is asking for his assistance are simply, 'I cannot do it!' Instead he gives *all* the credit to God, since it is God, not Joseph, who will give Pharaoh the answer. In addition, he re-emphasises the same point continually throughout his discourse:

> *'The dreams of Pharaoh are one and the same.* God has revealed *to Pharaoh what he is about to do ...* God has shown *Pharaoh what he is about to do ... The reason the dream was given to Pharaoh in two forms is that the matter has been firmly* decided by God, *and* God will do it *soon.'* (Gen. 41:25,28,32, emphases mine)

This four-fold repetition of the word 'God' reveals the inner attitude of Joseph's heart. Gone is the pride and self-centredness of the youthful dreamer; present is the humility and God-centredness of the mature prophet.

Joseph clearly didn't believe in 'open theism': that somehow God doesn't yet know the future. No! Joseph's God not only knows the future, He reveals it to His servants and is providentially working to see that these events come to pass.

This revelation of the sovereignty of God as the Lord of history, and the fact that Joseph clearly knows that this God is speaking to him, highlights a further significant lesson for us...

Exercise the gifts in faith and with boldness

Once we are operating in love and walking with a humble God-confidence, we are called to step out and speak out or serve with appropriate courage. Humble though Joseph may have been, he certainly wasn't timid. Whether before Pharaoh's officials or Pharaoh himself, Joseph demonstrated remarkable faith in the gift of God and displayed a tremendous boldness in exercising it. Having heard the dreams of the cupbearer and baker, he simply prefaced his interpretation with the phrase, 'This is what it means'. His confidence was well-founded. The cupbearer was restored to his position and the baker was killed: 'just as Joseph had said to them in his interpretation' (Gen. 40:22). Similarly, there is no hesitating or flinching before Pharaoh. Joseph simply but boldly speaks out what God has shown him.

Such boldness is vital if we are to exercise fully the gifts God has given us. Many would readily agree that we need to humble ourselves before God, but not so easily accept the need to then be bold for Him! But the one precedes and is foundational for the other. True humility will result in great boldness.

This is not a recommendation for an immature flaunting of gifts. Neither am I saying that we must preface everything with, 'Thus saith the Lord', especially if we are still growing in our ability to hear God. There is clearly a time for developing in the gifts and the picture we see of Joseph is of a young man still in his late twenties, but clearly mature in character and gifting. But boldness is a key in faithfully delivering the Word of God. This boldness includes a willingness to deliver the whole truth, not just the parts that people want to hear. It was probably much easier for Joseph to deliver to the cupbearer the following message:

'Within three days Pharaoh will lift up your head and restore you to your position, and you will put Pharaoh's cup in his hand, just as you used to do when you were his cupbearer.' (Gen. 40:13)

But it took far more courage to faithfully interpret the dream of the baker:

'Within three days Pharaoh will lift off your head and impale your body on a pole. And the birds will eat away your flesh.' (Gen. 40:19)

I wonder what the atmosphere in that prison was like during the following three days!

Even greater courage was needed to deliver a message of impending famine to the most powerful ruler of the day. But Joseph didn't stop there –

he had the boldness to go on and tell Pharaoh what to do as a result. He didn't say, 'Let me leave this with you...' he gave Pharaoh a plan of action, too.

Such boldness is vital for us today. While we are not necessarily called to be prophets like Joseph, we are all gifted, and are all called to step out and use our gifts boldly. Sometimes this may mean telling people the truth and the whole truth, even if it is unpalatable. I know for myself as a leader and preacher there can be a tendency to emphasise only the nice parts of the Bible. However, if we are to be true to the Lord and truly helpful to people, we must maintain a healthy balance between the 'fear of the Lord' and the 'comfort of the Holy Spirit' (Acts 9:31, NKJV), and be prepared both to challenge and encourage. This can mean, in particular, that we have to overcome our natural desire to be loved and accepted by others, and to resist the subtle snare of the fear of man. Only then can we be free to minister the gift with appropriate boldness. Regularly, we need to pray the prayer of the first apostles who, in the face of persecution, didn't back off but prayed:

> 'Now, Lord, consider their threats and enable your servants to speak your word with great boldness. *Stretch out your hand to heal and perform signs and wonders through the name of your holy servant Jesus.*' (Acts 4:29–30, emphasis mine)

Evidently, the Lord liked their prayer for:

> '*After they prayed, the place where they were meeting was shaken. And they were all filled with the Holy Spirit and spoke the word of God boldly.*' (Acts 4:31)

This emphasis on speaking the Word boldly needs to be tempered with a word of caution. Especially as we are developing our character and our prophetic gift, it is best to err on the side of encouragement rather than correction, and it is important to be aware that for New Testament believers, prophecy is primarily for 'strengthening, encouraging and comfort' (1 Cor. 14:3). Also, we must always speak the truth 'in love' (Eph. 4:15). For those who are mature leaders and who are called to exercise an apostolic, prophetic or teaching ministry, we must be prepared to preach the whole counsel of God, but do so in a way that is as wise and as winsome as possible.

As you faithfully exercise the gifts that God has given you, you can be confident that, in His timing and in His way, He will ensure that you will walk in the destiny that He has planned for you. But if you are to really break through into all that the Lord has for you, then you must firmly grasp a further vital truth...

You are gifted for Mondays and not just for Sundays!

While Joseph's prophetic gift gave him a platform before Pharaoh, it was his gifts of leadership and administration that kept him there. This is so important. Whereas some in the Church today minimise the prophetic and charismatic gifts as something confined to Bible times or to the establishment of the Church in the first few centuries, others overemphasise them to the exclusion of other more 'practical' gifts.

Some of the roots of this go back to the gnostic teaching of the first few centuries AD, which overplayed the 'spiritual' side of life at the expense of the 'natural' or 'physical'. Aspects of a secular/sacred divide also crept into the teaching of the medieval church. Instead of a New Testament model of every member in ministry, equipped by gifted leaders, there arose a false divide between the priests and the laity, with the former being the only 'real' ministers. During the Reformation in the early sixteenth century, Martin Luther and other reformers attacked this unbiblical world-view and argued strongly for the 'priesthood of all believers'. They contended for the right of all believers to come before God as 'priests' in worship and in service, and for the sanctity of ministry in the world of business, commerce, agriculture, medicine and education etc. Yet, tragically, five hundred years later, some churches and believers still have not grasped this vital concept. It is time for the whole Church to be reformed again, with every believer both ministering with their gifts in and through the life of the local church, but also employing their God-given gifts to serve His purposes in and through the family and then into their place of work. Remember, the Holy Spirit does not just anoint us for Sundays, but for Mondays, too!

Once again we can learn from Joseph. He was both prophet and planner, dreamer and leader. While there is no doubt that his gift of dream-interpretation was vital for getting him before Pharaoh, it was his leadership gift that kept him there. If we return to the Genesis account, we see that it was not simply that Joseph gave Pharaoh the meaning of his dreams, but he also gave him a practical solution as to what to do next:

> *'And now let Pharaoh look for a discerning and wise man and put him in charge of the land of Egypt. Let Pharaoh appoint commissioners over the land to take a fifth of the harvest of Egypt during the seven years of abundance. They should collect all the food of these good years that are coming and store up the grain under the authority of Pharaoh, to be kept in the cities for food. This food should be held in reserve for the country, to be used during the seven years of famine that will come upon Egypt, so that the country may not be ruined by the famine.'*
> (Gen. 41:33–36)

Here is Joseph, a lowly Hebrew slave just out of prison, delivering a 14-year strategic plan to the most powerful man in the world!

> *'The plan seemed good to Pharaoh and to all his officials. So Pharaoh asked them, "Can we find anyone like this man, one in whom is the spirit of God?" Then Pharaoh said to Joseph, "Since God has made all this known to you, there is no one so discerning and wise as you. You shall be in charge of my palace, and all my people are to submit to your orders. Only with respect to the throne will I be greater than you."'*
> (Gen. 41:37–40)

It is so important to see that it was 'the plan' that sufficiently impressed the court and led to Joseph's dramatic promotion. Had Joseph just stopped at the interpretation of the dream, he may well have been handsomely rewarded and promoted to be chief among Pharaoh's magicians, since none of his existing magicians had been able to interpret the dream (Gen. 41:24). But it is highly unlikely that Pharaoh would have entrusted the running of his entire empire to someone who was just a dream interpreter.

So, we too need to realise that as valuable and vital as the prophetic and other 'charismatic' gifts are, there are also other vital gifts that God gives that we must use if we are to be truly useful to Him and make a mark for Him in the tough world of work. Without the prophetic gift, Joseph would have still been in prison, but without the practical leadership gift, he would have never become ruler under Pharaoh. This is why it is so vital that both in the Church and in our own individual lives, we remove any false division between the sacred and the secular, and realise that all God's gifts are important.

Interestingly, apart from Joseph's dream at the age of 17, and his interpretation of the dreams of Pharaoh and his two servants when we was still no older than 30, we have no record of Joseph ever exercising his prophetic gift at any other time in his life. This does not mean that he didn't, but the emphasis shifts from him being a dreamer to a leader. Ultimately, it was as a leader and a politician that he became a world-changer, fulfilling God's saving purpose both for his own people and for the Egyptian empire.

Significantly, it was this gift of leadership and administration that first got the attention of Potiphar and the prison warder. It was his ability to get things done and to make things happen that impressed the 'men of the world'. It was this same ability that ultimately caused Pharaoh not just to promote Joseph but, more remarkably, to keep him at the pinnacle of power for the next 80 years. Pharaoh and his officials recognised, more than many Christians do, that the 'Spirit of God' was the inspiration for the plan and not just for the prophecy!

In every sphere of life we need both these elements. Any church or organisation needs a vision, a God-given dream. But there are many dreamers who never end up living the dream or seeing much happen due to the absence of a plan or the ability to implement one. No government or successful business just bumbles along on a day-to-day basis wondering what to do next. Rather, they normally have some kind of plan, whether short, medium or long term. Sadly, I have observed that many church leaders in the name of being 'Spirit-led' and 'prophetic' shun the need for planning. But the result is that not much is built of a long-term, sustainable nature. From experience, observation, and the wonderful example of Joseph, I would like to encourage all Christian leaders, be it in the church or the marketplace, to seek God for the vision, the plan *and* the successful implementation of that plan – and to believe that the Holy Spirit will inspire the whole process. To take the local church as an example, the wonderful truth is that as a body, no one person possesses or needs to possess all the gifts. Instead, we can learn to work together. In a leadership or ministry team there may well be those with a stronger leaning towards vision, others who are stronger in strategic planning, and others who are more gifted in administration and implementation. The overall lesson is that, if we work together, with everyone functioning in their sphere of maximum effectiveness towards the common goal, then the Church will truly begin to impact the world.

As Christians allow the Holy Spirit to anoint them for strategic leadership roles, so we will see a whole new generation of 'Josephs': high-level influencers in the marketplace. We will start seeing Christian politicians, business leaders, head teachers, lawyers and doctors affecting society with genuine kingdom values and, like Joseph, helping to fulfil the strategic purposes of God both for the Church and for the world around. God used Joseph to provide salvation to the known world! And He wants to use you and me to be a storehouse of blessing too. We won't do this alone. But as we work together as the Church of Jesus Christ, recognising and faithfully exercising the gifts He has given us, we can help change the world.

CHAPTER 7

BLESSED TO BE A BLESSING

Joseph's promotion was sudden and staggering. In a single day the prisoner became 'Prime Minister'. Having passed the tests of preparation, he now faced the challenges of prosperity. Handling success is sometimes much harder than handling failure. In the words of J. Oswald Sanders, 'Not every man can carry a full cup. Sudden elevation frequently leads to pride and a fall. The most exacting test of all to survive is prosperity.'[4]

Yet Joseph passed the prosperity test just as he had passed the adversity test, with flying colours. He is a great example to us all of how God can elevate a man and give him extraordinary influence and affluence without it ruining him in the process. There are a number of vital lessons that we can learn, the first of which is this…

Acknowledge God as the source of the blessing

Joseph's promotion clearly came from God. Stephen is quite clear about this:

> '[God] gave Joseph wisdom *and enabled him to gain the goodwill of Pharaoh king of Egypt. So Pharaoh made him ruler over Egypt and all his palace.*' (Acts 7:10, emphasis mine)

The speed and scale of Joseph's elevation are quite outstanding, with authority second only to Pharaoh himself. Along with this came incredible influence and affluence:

> '*So Pharaoh said to Joseph, "I hereby put you in charge of the whole land of Egypt." Then Pharaoh took his signet ring from his finger and put it on Joseph's finger. He dressed him in robes of fine linen and put a gold chain round his neck. He made him ride in a chariot as his second-in-command, and people shouted before him, "Make way!" Thus he put him in charge of the whole land of Egypt.*' (Gen. 41:41–43)

There were a number of symbols of this newfound power. First, there was Pharaoh's own signet ring. This was equivalent to him giving Joseph his credit card. Second, there were robes of fine linen and a gold necklace, symbols of the huge personal wealth that Joseph would now enjoy. Third, there was a chariot, indicating that he was second-in-command – a bit like a vice-presidential limousine!

There is no suggestion that this remarkable blessing was something evil, rather it was a gift to Joseph from the providential hand of his God. Some people would have problems fitting this into their theology. While the Bible nowhere guarantees power or riches for all, this remarkable story does emphasise that God still wants to promote modern day 'Josephs' to fulfil His sovereign purposes on the earth. Commenting on this in his study on Joseph, Charles Swindoll asks:

> *'But what of the person who does survive [the prosperity test], honouring God with his or her wealth? Does the evangelical church today embrace that man or woman? Is there room in the pew for someone who is obviously blessed with this world's goods? Or is that person unwelcome because of envy or jealousy or resentment?'*[5]

So, what should our perspective be concerning material wealth and possessions?

Seek first God's kingdom

There is much teaching throughout the Bible on this important subject, not least in the Gospels. One of the most helpful summaries is found in Matthew chapter 6, where Jesus deals with materialism on the one hand and worrying about insufficiency on the other. He concludes with a masterful summary:

'But seek first his kingdom and his righteousness, and all these things will be given to you as well.' (Matt. 6:33)

Here we have Jesus' perspective in a nutshell. Material wealth should never be our goal or focus in life, but rather God's kingdom and His righteousness. When we put 'first things first' then there is a corresponding blessing and 'all these things' (clearly, in this context, material provision), will be added to us, not just for ourselves, but for others, too.

A similar perspective is found in 1 Timothy 6. On the one hand, Paul clearly warns of the grave dangers of greed and materialism:

'Those who want to get rich fall into temptation and a trap and into many foolish and harmful desires that plunge people into ruin and destruction. For the love of money is a root of all kinds of evil. Some people, eager for money, have wandered from the faith and pierced themselves with many griefs.' (vv9–10)

The warning is not against money but rather the 'love of money' and of being 'eager for' ('reaching after' or 'grasping at') wealth. Falling into this temptation can start a downward spiral of being trapped by the devil, consumed by foolish desires and ultimately plunged into ruin and destruction, both in this life and in eternity. Yet, Paul also gives us hope that we can escape from this trap by embracing the principle of contentment:

'But godliness with contentment is great gain. For we brought nothing into the world, and we can take nothing out of it. But if we have food and clothing, we will be content with that.' (1 Tim. 6:6–8)

There is great blessing in contentment, as the following story illustrates:

One day, a fisherman was lying on a beautiful beach with his fishing pole propped up in the sand and his solitary line cast out into the sparkling blue surf. He was enjoying the warmth of the afternoon sun and the prospect of catching a fish. About that time, a businessman came walking down the beach, trying to relieve some of the stress of his workday. He noticed the fisherman sitting on the beach and said, 'You should be working rather than lying on the beach!'

The fisherman looked up at the businessman, smiled and replied, 'And what will my reward be?'

'Well, you can get bigger nets and catch more fish!' was the businessman's answer.

'And then what will my reward be?' asked the fisherman, still smiling.

The businessman replied, 'You will make money and you'll be able to buy a boat, which will then result in larger catches of fish!'

'And then what will my reward be?' asked the fisherman again.

The businessman was beginning to get a little irritated with the fisherman's questions. 'You can buy a bigger boat, and hire some people to work for you!' he said.

'And then what will my reward be?' repeated the fisherman.

The businessman was getting angry. 'Don't you understand? You can build up a fleet of fishing boats, sail all over the world, and let all your employees catch fish for you!'

Once again the fisherman asked, 'And then what will my reward be?'

The businessman was red with rage and shouted at the fisherman, 'Don't you understand that you can become so rich that you won't have to work for your living again! You can spend all the rest of your days sitting on this beach, looking at the sunset. You won't have a care in the world!' The fisherman, still smiling, looked up and said, 'And what do you think I'm doing right now?'

I use this story not to encourage idleness (since there are plenty of biblical exhortations for hard work leading to prosperity), but rather to highlight the need for contentment.

But what if someone is (like Joseph) already rich? Here the exhortation again concerns right heart attitudes:

'Tell those who are rich not to be proud and not to trust in their money, which will soon be gone, but their pride and trust should be in the living God who always richly gives us all we need for our enjoyment. Tell them to use their money to do good. They should be rich in good works and should give happily to those in need, always being ready to share with others whatever God has given them. By doing this they will be storing up real treasure for themselves in heaven—it is the only safe investment for eternity!' (1 Tim. 6:17–19, TLB)

So, the balanced teaching is this: don't make wealth your ultimate goal. If God has entrusted you with material wealth, don't allow your blessings to make you arrogant or trust in your riches, but trust in God, who is the source of these blessings. Moreover, recognise that you have been given a responsibility to be generous and to invest in the lives of others, which will in turn secure an even greater 'investment' in eternity. This highlights how important it is to...

Be a good steward of what you have been given

All of us have been given a portion of time, talents and treasure that God expects us to manage well. Whether we feel we have been given much or little, we are all called to faithfully steward what the Lord has entrusted to us. This will require us to cultivate an attitude of diligence. Again we can learn from Joseph, a man who didn't waste his opportunity but was diligent in the administration of his duties. We read how:

'Joseph went throughout the land of Egypt. Joseph was thirty years old when he entered the service of Pharaoh king of Egypt. And Joseph went out from Pharaoh's presence and travelled throughout Egypt. During the seven years of abundance the land produced plentifully. Joseph collected all the food produced in those seven years of abundance in

*Egypt and stored it in the cities. In each city he put the food grown
in the fields surrounding it. Joseph stored up huge quantities of grain,
like the sand of the sea; it was so much that he stopped keeping records
because it was beyond measure.'* (Gen. 41:45–49)

The first thing we see here is that Joseph served Pharaoh well. As he
had demonstrated earlier, Joseph turned out to be a great 'second chair
leader'. He was diligent and faithful to carry out the plan. The double
reference to him travelling 'throughout the land' suggests a 'hands-on'
approach and a genuine interest in the people of the land. He was in
the 'service of Pharaoh', but was determined to serve the people well,
too. There seems also to be an emphasis placed on the fact that it was
Joseph himself who 'collected all the food' and 'stored up huge quantities
of grain'. This doesn't mean he was physically involved in implementing
these decisions – instead he worked through 'commissioners' (41:34) –
but the text is showing us that here was a man who could be trusted to
get the job done. No wonder he was such an asset to anyone he worked for.

But Joseph was not just efficient, he was also highly effective. He was
not just wandering aimlessly around Egypt trying to look busy, he was
purposefully working to implement a plan. The plan, as we have seen,
flowed out of the prophetic interpretation of Pharaoh's dream and was a
plan for the whole nation:

*'Let Pharaoh appoint commissioners over the land to take a fifth of
the harvest of Egypt during the seven years of abundance. They should
collect all the food of these good years that are coming and store up
the grain under the authority of Pharaoh, to be kept in the cities for
food. This food should be held in reserve for the country, to be used
during the seven years of famine that will come upon Egypt, so that the
country may not be ruined by the famine.'* (Gen. 41:34–36)

The plan focused on saving up grain during a time of surplus. Without such
a plan, when the famine came, millions would have starved. Today, it is still

vital for governments and business leaders to plan ahead if they are to thrive economically. The same applies to churches and individuals. If we don't have a plan and a corresponding budget, or at least guiding principles, we will be at the mercy of every whim or latest 'need' that comes our way and as a result we will not prosper.

Moreover, Joseph's 'savings plan' provides a salutary lesson to us today. In 2008, much of the world experienced a severe economic recession, the root of which was reckless lending by the banks to those who couldn't afford to pay back. But there was a deeper root to this crisis: the 'borrow and spend' philosophy that lies at the heart of so much of modern day materialism. The old fashioned disciplines of budgeting, saving and spending only what you can afford had, for many years, been thrown out and the consequences are now all around us. Whether governments, businesses or individuals, reckless spending based on credit has got to stop.

Let's learn from Joseph. Not only did he propose and implement a basic principle of saving and storing up during a time of abundance, but he saved more than was strictly necessary. By saving a fifth of the harvest during the whole seven years, he ensured that the storehouses were filled with more than enough when the famine came, not just for the nation of Egypt but also for surrounding nations, including Joseph's own family. His diligent and effective stewardship of the responsibility he had been given is an inspiration to anyone serving in marketplace ministry.

Be 'in' but not 'of' the world

Sadly, many Christians who get promoted 'in the world' then end up becoming part 'of the world'. In other words, they forget the source of their blessing and allow the value system of the world around them to set their guiding principles. But Joseph, it seems, managed to be in Egypt without letting too much of Egypt contaminate him. It was not that Joseph avoided becoming immersed in the culture of his day. We read that:

'Pharaoh gave Joseph the name Zaphenath-Paneah and gave him Asenath daughter of Potiphera, priest of On, to be his wife. And Joseph went throughout the land of Egypt.' (Gen. 41:45)

Joseph was given an Egyptian name that meant 'God has spoken and he lives'. So, even his 'worldly' name was a means of God receiving glory. Like Daniel centuries later, God seems to have been OK with His 'man-on-the-inside' taking on some outward signs of the surrounding culture. But in any case, Joseph the former Hebrew slave and prisoner presumably didn't have much choice in the matter. He probably didn't have much say about who he was to marry either – his wife was daughter of the priest of On, one of the most powerful families in Egypt. And his travelling throughout Egypt (mentioned twice in the text), may partly have been to acquaint himself fully with the new people whom he had been given responsibility for.

The question is, in all of this did Joseph compromise? With regard to the change of name and the decision to travel, the answer is surely 'no'. In fact, there is a very positive lesson here. If we are going to truly influence the culture we live in, we must understand it and get involved in it. We are not called as Christians to be completely segregated from, or even fearful of life around us, but rather to be 'in' but not 'of' the world.

However, the matter of Joseph marrying into an Egyptian priestly family is more problematic. The broader counsel of the Scriptures is that intermarriage for God's people is clearly wrong. Earlier in Genesis, the narrator had gone to significant lengths to highlight the importance of Isaac and Jacob not marrying a daughter of the Canaanites (Gen. 24:3–4; 28:1). Later, under the Law, intermarriage was strictly forbidden and those who violated these principles, such as King Solomon or the exiles under Ezra and Nehemiah, were clearly portrayed as disobedient to God. In the New Testament, Paul was keen to point out the broader principle of the dangers of being 'unequally yoked' with unbelievers.

Can I strongly urge you: if you are a committed Christian and considering dating, let alone marrying someone who is not also committed to Christ, then don't do it! Not only is it against the general teachings of Scripture, but experience would suggest that it can be a cause of untold pain to be married to someone who cannot share your faith. Moreover, the 'hope' that they might eventually become a Christian is usually unfounded. The reverse often happens, with the unsaved partner dragging their spouse away from their faith.

So, what are we to make of Joseph's marriage? Clearly, this exception doesn't violate the broader scriptural principles. Moreover, the narrator's lack of comment on the situation doesn't necessarily imply approval. Rather, having an Egyptian wife was a non-negotiable part of the package of working for Pharaoh. This was combined with the fact that Joseph was in Egypt and so presumably had no other worshippers of Yahweh that he could marry at the time.

Perhaps more significantly, Joseph, unlike Solomon, didn't allow his wife to turn his heart after other gods. This is strikingly demonstrated in the naming of his sons:

> 'Joseph named his firstborn Manasseh and said, "It is because God has made me forget all my trouble and all my father's household." The second son he named Ephraim and said, "It is because God has made me fruitful in the land of my suffering."' (Gen. 41:51–52)

In spite of being in Egypt, serving a powerful Egyptian pharaoh and being married into a priestly Egyptian family, Joseph ensured that his boys were given thoroughly Hebrew names! And their names were both in direct honour of God. Manasseh sounds like and may be derived from the Hebrew for 'forget', whereas Ephraim sounds like the Hebrew word for 'twice fruitful'. Both names were given to acknowledge that Joseph's newfound promotion and prosperity had come from the God of Abraham, Isaac and Jacob. Given the significance of both names and descendants in the Near Eastern world, this was as powerful a statement as Joseph could have made that his true allegiance was still with the God of his forefathers. Despite being very much in Egypt, he was clearly still a worshipper of the one true God, and on this fundamental truth he was not prepared to compromise. As a covenant man he knew the source of his newfound elevation and prosperity and was prepared to acknowledge it. This leads us to a final point...

Be blessed to be a blessing

Joseph was undoubtedly blessed, but he was primarily blessed to be a blessing, first to Egypt and then to the covenant people of God. He was lifted up not so that he could selfishly live the dream for his own life, but in order to fulfil the strategic purposes of God in history, bringing salvation both to Israel and to Egypt. For us, too, God wants to promote us individually and the Church collectively, not for our own selfish agenda, but in order to fulfil His redemptive purposes in the earth. In doing so we are fulfilling the original mandate given to Joseph's great-grandfather and our 'father in the faith', Abraham:

> *'I will bless you ... and you will be a blessing. I will bless those who bless you ... and all peoples on earth will be blessed through you.'*
> (Gen. 12:2–3)

This was what Joseph's original dream was all about. God providentially foresaw a need and provided a man to help meet that need. Having been given both the interpretation and application of Pharaoh's dreams of forthcoming famine, Joseph was then entrusted with the task of rescuing the world from starvation. The narrator records:

> *'The seven years of abundance in Egypt came to an end, and the seven years of famine began, just as Joseph had said. There was famine in all the other lands, but in the whole land of Egypt there was food. When all Egypt began to feel the famine, the people cried to Pharaoh for food. Then Pharaoh told all the Egyptians, "Go to Joseph and do what he tells you."*

> *When the famine had spread over the whole country, Joseph opened all the storehouses and sold grain to the Egyptians, for the famine was severe throughout Egypt. And all the world came to Egypt to buy grain from Joseph, because the famine was severe everywhere.'*
> (Gen. 41:53–57)

Joseph is presented here as saviour of the world! Later, when being reconciled with his brothers he recognised the full import of his role:

> '*it was to* save lives *that God sent me ahead of you. For two years now there has been famine in the land, and for the next five years there will be no ploughing and reaping. But God sent me ahead of you to preserve for you a remnant on earth and* to save your lives by a great deliverance.' (Gen. 45:5–7, emphases mine)

The dreamer has matured and the dream is being fulfilled. Gone is the boasting of a prideful young man, interested primarily in his own elevation. In its place is a focus on the purpose of a sovereign God being fulfilled, bringing salvation to Israel and the nations.

So, how does this apply to us today? First, as 'saviour', Joseph is a forerunner of the greater Saviour, Jesus Christ, who having been betrayed by His own people was killed on a cross and then raised up and exalted to bring salvation first to His people, the Jews, and then to all the peoples of the earth. Joseph brought physical salvation and 'bread' for the peoples of his day, but only Jesus, the 'bread of life', can truly satisfy the deepest needs of humanity, both in this life and the next (John 6:35). Now, as Jesus' body on earth, we as the Church are called to bring the 'bread' of salvation to the ends of the earth. We are to present Him as the answer to the needs of all peoples everywhere. God used Joseph to provide salvation to the known world; He wants to use you and me to help change the whole world. In his book, *The Tide is Turning*, Terry Virgo highlights the role of the Church of Jesus Christ as a storehouse for the nations and how God has been preparing His Church ready to meet the needs of those around:

'In the last days, God will bring forth a marvellous, mature,
"Joseph company" with answers for the famine. People will stream in.'[6]

Today, God is in the process of strengthening His people, gathering them in strong local churches all across the planet to bring His salvation to their neighbourhoods and to the nations.

But there is a further lesson that we can learn from Joseph. God is not just concerned with the spiritual needs of humanity, but with its physical and material needs too. The famine of Joseph's day was a real economic and social disaster, and God called His man to provide the solution. If we are to be true 'Joseph companies' or modern day individual 'Josephs', then we need to be prepared to get involved in every aspect of helping our world which, although fallen, is ultimately God's world. We need to be reminded that we serve a Saviour who not only preached to people's spiritual and eternal needs but also 'went around doing good and healing all' who were oppressed by the devil (Acts 10:38). This will mean many things, such as healing the sick and helping the poor with food, clothing and aid, but it will also involve God promoting modern day 'Josephs' to positions of sometimes amazing influence and affluence, so that they can help deal with some of the causes as well as symptoms of human suffering. Such Christ-centred, humble but talented men and women will penetrate the world of politics, economics, business, education and health. Once in position they will fulfil their assignment, which is to start challenging the laws, policies and values of society from within, bringing the rule and reign of God into every sphere of life.

CHAPTER 8

RESTORING RELATIONSHIPS

So, what is the climax of Joseph's story? At first glance it may seem to be his spectacular promotion before Pharaoh, but this has been told by the end of Genesis 41 and there are still nine chapters of the story left. On closer inspection, the high-point is Joseph's reconciliation with his brothers in chapter 45, which leads in turn to the moving restoration of his relationship with his father in chapter 46. This is arguably one of the most dramatic and moving accounts of family reconciliation, not only in the entire inspired Scriptures, but also in human literature as a whole. As such, it provides great hope and many lessons for all who are currently caught in the devastating web of familial or relationship breakdown.

The importance of reconciliation and the restoration of relationships can be seen all around us. Two decades on from the end of apartheid, Nelson Mandela's example of forgiveness still shines brightly. Having visited Robben Island, I have been able to get a firsthand glimpse of the horror and suffering that he and his compatriots had to endure at the hands of the apartheid regime, a fact which makes his refusal to seek revenge all the more remarkable. It is widely recognised that it was his leadership that was instrumental in the relatively peaceful and harmonious transition to the post-apartheid era. His desire to forgive and offer reconciliation both to his captors and to the regime as a whole is one of the reasons why South Africa, with all its challenges, is still a place with a hope and a future.

Joseph, like Mandela, encourages us to be agents of reconciliation. In this chapter, we will focus on Genesis 42–44 and the process leading up to relational restoration. In the next chapter, we will examine the high drama of Genesis 45 when the restoration actually takes place.

So why the need for the long drawn-out drama of Genesis 42–44, and what sense are we to make of three visits of the brothers to Egypt and of Joseph's two-year 'testing' of them? Other than the simple fact that the narrator is telling us what happened, why was this section so necessary for the story then and so important for us now?

First, this two-year period was a vital process of transformation for Joseph himself. By the end of Genesis 41 we see him at the pinnacle of power with seemingly unlimited resources and opportunities at his disposal. Yet the dream had still not become reality. While he may have already forgiven his brothers, he was still an exile in a foreign land and estranged from the rest of his family. With the unexpected arrival of his brothers in Egypt and them bowing down before him, the first of his dreams was fulfilled. Moreover, this event triggered a two-year process in which Joseph was able to witness firsthand their evolving change of heart, sufficient for him to risk trusting them again and initiate full-scale reconciliation.

Second, this two-year process was essential for the family. God had a hugely significant future for Jacob's descendants: together with Joseph's two sons, the sons of Jacob would become the 12 tribes of Israel. Yet, in order to fulfil this high calling they had to be brought back from the brink of betrayal and deception through a process of genuine repentance. In particular, the fourth son of Jacob, Judah, was called to become the forefather of the Messiah and so his emergence as a repentant and transformed leader was vital for the future history of God's redemptive plans.

Third, this whole section can be seen as a powerful foreshadowing of the person and work of Jesus. Both Judah, through his offer of intercession and substitution, and Joseph, betrayed and yet granting forgiveness to his brothers, can be seen as 'types' of the promised Messiah.

Fourth, these events are of major encouragement to us today. If in any way we are currently suffering from unresolved conflict and relationship breakdown, these chapters give us hope for a better future. In a world where we see the devastating effects of sin on family life and human relationships all around, these chapters encourage us to seek forgiveness, reconciliation and healing.

The particular text we will be studying, Genesis 42–44, is the longest and most involved section of the entire narrative. Most studies and commentaries do a chapter by chapter analysis and, of course, there is benefit to this. The downside, however, is that one can easily get lost in the intricacies of the plot and miss the broader message that is coming through. So, rather than adopting a simple chronological approach, we will be embarking on a character analysis of the key players: Joseph, the brothers, Jacob and God Himself. This will enable us to focus on the main theme of reconciliation and of how we can apply this to our lives today.

Joseph: greatly sinned against

Joseph is a great example to us of how we are to respond to those who have sinned against us, particularly when that sin has caused us significant pain and suffering. So how did Joseph react? Walter Brueggemann has suggested that Joseph's two-year 'testing' of his brothers was borne out of a desire for revenge:

> 'He is presented as ruthless, cunning and vengeful. He is prepared to return to his brothers some of the grief caused him. He has forgotten nothing. There is nothing noble about him. There is no hint that he has any awareness of a larger vocation.'[7]

Others authors argue the opposite. Robert Candlish presents Joseph as so full of mercy that he wanted to reveal his identity immediately, but was restrained by God who was using his 'testing' to bring true repentance and salvation for his brothers.[8] Along similar lines, Liam Goligher summarises how, on seeing his brothers:

> 'Joseph remembers his dream and suddenly he realises that their arrival in Egypt is no coincidence, it is the hand of God. He remembers his role as God's servant ... Joseph is not looking for revenge, nor does he punish anyone. He tests his brothers to see whether he can trust them and to find out whether there has been any change in attitude. He is used by God to bring them to repentance and a real change of mind, heart and action.'[9]

So is Joseph an offended, ruthless individual exacting revenge, or is he a forgiving, humble servant, deliberately carrying out the sovereign purposes of his saving God? Or is there a third alternative? Is he someone who has basically forgiven his brothers many years ago but now, faced with the prospect of reconciliation, is demonstrating a need to discern the genuineness of their repentance before trusting them again? In other words, this story may not be about someone who is deliberately exacting human revenge or consciously effecting divine transformation: rather, it is about someone who wants to be reconciled with his family, but wants to make sure that the reconciliation will be genuine and lasting, and who in the process of doing so, maybe consciously, is carrying out the 'hidden plans' of God. If that is the case, then it teaches us, too, some vital principles about how we can be instrumental in being reconciled with those who have hurt or offended us.

As we seek to learn lessons from Joseph about the journey of rebuilding trust, it is interesting to try and imagine what his first reaction would have been when he first saw his brothers in Egypt. Twenty years after the initial betrayal, he was now face to face with his abusers. They were unaware of who he was and bowing down as in the dream:

> '*So when Joseph's brothers arrived, they bowed down to him with their faces to the ground. As soon as Joseph saw his brothers, he recognised them, but he pretended to be a stranger and spoke harshly to them. "Where do you come from?" he asked. "From the land of Canaan," they replied, "to buy food." Although Joseph recognised his brothers, they did not recognise him. Then he remembered his dreams about them*' (Gen. 42:6–9)

Some who have been abused long for such an opportunity to face their abusers and wonder how they would respond. Significantly, in this initial encounter, Joseph was not ready to either confront or to be reconciled. Rather, from this advantageous position he first tested his brothers' integrity, accusing them three times of being spies, before requiring that they return with their absent brother, Benjamin, while he detained Simeon as a hostage.

Lest we see this as an example of a vengeful attitude we need to note that his testing of them is accompanied by a desire to save their family from starvation. Not only does he load them up with grain for their return journey to Canaan but, as they later discover, he has also returned their silver in full. Certainly this represented a further test of their integrity and was maybe directly linked to the fact that they had sold Joseph into slavery for 20 shekels of silver. But it also surely represented the generosity of Joseph, since he had no guarantee that they would return.

Joseph's generosity was further highlighted following the brothers' return visit to Egypt. On seeing his own younger brother Benjamin with them, Joseph immediately orders his steward:

'Take these men to my house, slaughter an animal and prepare a meal; they are to eat with me at noon.' (Gen. 43:16)

The harshness of their first encounter seemed to have disappeared. Moreover, terrified at the prospect of going to this powerful man's house, they confessed to the steward the saga of the silver and offered to pay it back, only to receive the following response:

'"It's all right," he said. "Don't be afraid. Your God, the God of your father, has given you treasure in your sacks; I received your silver." Then he brought Simeon out to them.' (Gen. 43:23)

This remarkable reaction from an Egyptian steward can only be explained if he had previously been briefed by his master, Joseph. The double mention of 'God', the 'God of your father', must have come from Joseph, which strongly suggests that Joseph was already very conscious of the guiding hand of God in this whole process. This non-return of the silver, coupled with the release of Simeon, indicated that mercy was triumphing over judgment!

The transformation in Joseph is striking. The selfish, prideful boasting of the young dreamer has now been replaced by a genuine concern for the welfare of others. At the point of the dream being fulfilled, with the brothers bowing down before him, there is a conspicuous absence of any gloating. Rather, Joseph's immediate response was to ask about the wellbeing of their father, before being evidently moved by the sight of his younger brother who he hadn't seen for over twenty years:

> 'As he looked about and saw his brother Benjamin, his own mother's son, he asked, "Is this your youngest brother, the one you told me about?" And he said, "God be gracious to you, my son." Deeply moved at the sight of his brother, Joseph hurried out and looked for a place to weep. He went into his private room and wept there. After he had washed his face, he came out and, controlling himself, said, "Serve the food."' (Gen. 43:29–31)

This very moving scene not only opens a window into Joseph's true feelings, it also emphasises the importance of reconciliation and relational restoration. Joseph may well have been able to forgive his brothers 20 years previously, but the absence of his family had still left a void in his life. Although by many standards he was already living the dream, enjoying the blessing of God and experiencing tremendous influence and affluence, there was something distinctly unfulfilled and incomplete in his personal life. It was not until the family was reconciled and together again that the dream was truly fulfilled.

Although the process of restoration was underway, Joseph was still not ready to reveal himself. Instead, the sight of his younger brother, Benjamin, provided the occasion for a feast of generosity, which in turn gave opportunity for Joseph to again witness the attitude of his brothers. In giving Benjamin five times the portion of any of the others, he was not only showing his love for his long lost brother, but was checking to see how the others would respond. After all, it had been their jealousy at their father's favouritism towards Joseph that had torn the family in two. How would the brothers respond to another instance of clear favouritism? The answer, it seems, was very positively:

'So they feasted and drank freely with [Benjamin].' (Gen. 43:34)

There is no sign of any jealousy here, but rather a genuine rejoicing at their family blessing and at the special favour that their young brother had been given.

But Joseph was still to be convinced and so he arranged one final test, deliberately ordering that his special cup be hidden in Benjamin's sack. Twenty years after rejecting and disowning Joseph, would they act differently towards his younger brother? Judah's initial response on behalf of the brothers was telling:

'We are now my lord's slaves – we ourselves and the one who was found to have the cup.' (Gen. 44:16)

All for one and one for all! Moreover, Joseph's suggestion that only Benjamin would be punished was the trigger for the dramatic intercession and offer of substitution from Judah (see next section), which was the final indication that the repentance was wholehearted and that the brothers could be trusted again. It was this that finally prompted Joseph to reveal himself.

So what are we to learn from Joseph's 'testing' of his brothers? First, it is important to note that this is a unique story with its own personalities and circumstances and we must be careful not to draw too many exact parallels to our own situations. The narrator is first and foremost narrating, without necessarily making moral or theological comments as to the rights or wrongs of a particular course of action. It would clearly be unwise to draw inappropriate conclusions, for example by assuming that the best way to initiate reconciliation with others is to secretly set up a whole series of tests for those who have offended us! Rather, we must learn the importance of pursuing relational reconciliation, while recognising that it takes wisdom and often a period of time for this to properly take effect.

It is also necessary to re-emphasise that there is a big difference between forgiveness and reconciliation. As we have seen in Chapter 2, there is sufficient evidence to suggest that years earlier Joseph had forgiven those who had offended him, be it his brothers, Mrs Potiphar or the cupbearer. The absence of any sign of bitterness and the continued presence and blessing of God on his life, suggests that, as much as is humanly possible, Joseph had been able to move on and not let resentment from the past hold him back. So, for us too! If we have been offended, hurt, sinned against or abused, we can forgive our offender, even if they are not physically present or are still unrepentant, and by so doing can live free from that offence and carry on a normal, successful, healthy life, enjoying the grace of God.

However forgiveness, while vital, is only the first step in the process of restoration. Once we have forgiven someone before God we must, wherever possible, press through to relational reconciliation with the person(s) concerned. Yet this often takes time, especially where the offence has been more serious. Significantly, three of the 13 chapters of the Genesis story (a quarter if you subtract chapter 38 on Judah), are about this *process* of testing and repentance, and a whole other chapter details the actual reconciliation. This is not, as Brueggemann has suggested, because Joseph is getting his pound of flesh in revenge. Neither is it just because it takes that amount of time for genuine repentance on the part of the brothers, as crucial as this was. Rather, it is because it takes time for the offended party, Joseph, to become fully convinced of the brothers' change of heart and for trust to be rebuilt before he is ready to initiate genuine reconciliation.

The brothers: who have greatly sinned

It is one thing to seek reconciliation if we are the offended party, but what if we, like the brothers, are the ones who are guilty of the offence, especially if our sin seems great and has caused much harm to those involved?

It is worth at this stage remembering the gravity of the brothers' sin. Out of hatred and jealousy they had nearly killed their own blood brother before selling him as a slave and then lying about his 'disappearance' to their grief-stricken father – a lie they maintained for almost two decades. Yet the good news is that they came to a place of true repentance, were forgiven, reconciled and restored, and so can we be, too!

First, however, we need to realise that sin does have serious consequences for all concerned. Brueggemann has suggested that two decades after the original offence:

> 'The brothers have no room in which to act, no energy for imagination, and no possibility of freedom. They are bound by an unforgiven past, immobilised by guilt, driven by anxiety'[10]

He cites as evidence their seeming passivity in the face of the famine:

> 'When Jacob learned that there was grain in Egypt, he said to his sons, "Why do you just keep looking at each other?" He continued, "I have heard that there is grain in Egypt. Go down there and buy some for us, so that we may live and not die." Then ten of Joseph's brothers went down to buy grain from Egypt.' (Gen. 42:1–3)

Whether it was passivity or a fear of going to the land where they had sold their brother to slavery, the important fact is that sin cripples. An unforgiven past, with its corresponding guilt, shame and deception, is a heavy load to bear. The brothers needed to go to Egypt not just to get grain for their physical survival, but also to meet Joseph and receive spiritual restoration!

Crucial to their restoration (and ours) was the need for repentance which, in turn, started with a growing awareness of their sin. In their first encounter with Joseph, where he accused them of being spies, they simply told the facts about their family:

*'they replied: "Your servants were twelve brothers, the sons of one man,
who lives in the land of Canaan. The youngest is now with our father,
and one is no more."'* (Gen. 42:13)

They told the truth, but not yet the whole truth. But having been put
into prison by Joseph for three days and then being told that one of them
must stay behind while the rest of them go and fetch Benjamin, their
consciences were awakened:

*'Surely we are being punished because of our brother. We saw how
distressed he was when he pleaded with us for his life, but we would not
listen; that's why this distress has come upon us.'* (Gen. 42:21)

Given that the betrayal of Joseph had happened nearly twenty years
ago, it is remarkable that their first response was to relate their present
predicament to their past sin. At the time they had seemed so callous
in throwing Joseph into a pit and then selling him into slavery. But sin
has a deeply scarring effect on all who commit it and it is impossible
to completely bury guilt.

However, an awareness of sin, while a good start, is not the same
as repentance. Rather than taking responsibility for their own actions,
the brothers first attempted to play the 'blame game':

*'Reuben replied, "Didn't I tell you not to sin against the boy? But you
wouldn't listen! Now we must give an accounting for his blood."'*
(Gen. 42:22)

Like Adam with his wife in the garden, so Reuben, the firstborn, tried to
shift the blame to his brothers.

Yet this sense of guilt was accompanied by a growing awareness
of divine retribution and that somehow the brothers were giving
'an accounting' for their actions. This fear of God was further increased
when, on their return to Canaan, they found to their horror that not

only were their bags filled with grain, but the silver they gave to pay for it had been returned as well. Again, their response is striking:

> 'Their hearts sank and they turned to each other trembling and said, "What is this that God has done to us?"' (Gen. 42:28)

Interestingly, it is this act of 'kindness' (albeit a test from Joseph) that first prompted a full acknowledgement that it was ultimately God who was the 'hidden hand' behind their testing. Similarly for us, often it is the mercy rather than the severity of God that can be decisive in our acknowledgement of His Lordship (see Rom. 2:4).

This unexpected turn of events seems to have had a fearful and humbling effect on the brothers, and they reported back to their father in an open and honest manner. Jacob's despairing response at the news of the 'loss' of Simeon and his determination not to release Benjamin, in turn provoked another interesting reaction from Reuben:

> 'You may put both of my sons to death if I do not bring him back to you. Entrust him to my care, and I will bring him back.' (Gen. 42:37)

At first glance this may look like the beginning of Reuben, the firstborn son, taking responsibility and showing leadership. However, on closer inspection, his potential sacrificing of his sons was a rash and selfish action. Later, Reuben was to be formally sidelined for having slept with his father's concubine (Gen. 49:4). His place was to be taken by the fourth son, Judah, who was being prepared to be forefather of kings and, ultimately, the Messiah (Gen. 49:10).

The transformation of Judah's character in chapters 43–44 is both historically significant and practically inspiring, showing how God can deal with the corrupt human heart. First, he had clearly played a leading role in Joseph's captivity:

*'Judah said to his brothers, "What will we gain if we kill our brother
and cover up his blood? Come, let's sell him to the Ishmaelites and not
lay our hands on him; after all, he is our brother, our own flesh and
blood." His brothers agreed.'* (Gen. 37:26–27)

Whether his actions were out of a genuine concern to save Joseph from
death or a cynical attempt to gain financially, he was instrumental in selling
his own brother and was fully involved in the deception against their father.

As so often happens, sin and the ensuing cover-up led to further sin.
The betrayal in chapter 37 was followed by further deceit and sexual
immorality in chapter 38. How does a person get to such a low point in
life? Usually through a clear act of disobedience, which opens the door
to sin and the devil. In Judah's case it seems to have been his decision,
in direct contrast to the example of his forefathers, to marry a Canaanite
woman. From the outset this produced bad fruit: his first two sons
from this union were so wicked that the Lord had to put them to death.
Judah then compounded his sin by failing to honour his promise to
give his younger son to his widowed daughter-in-law, Tamar. She in
turn decided to take matters into her own hands, disguising herself
as a 'prostitute', presumably knowing her father-in-law's fondness for
fornicating in this way. True to form, Judah sought out a prostitute and
slept with her. On hearing news that his daughter-in-law had become a
prostitute and was now pregnant (by him!) he hypocritically called for
her to be burned to death, before being faced with the truth of his own
sin. The contrast between the unrighteousness of Judah towards Tamar
in chapter 38 and the righteousness of Joseph towards Potiphar's wife
in chapter 39 could hardly have been greater.

In the light of his sordid past, Judah's repentance was vital on a number
of levels: first, as the forefather of the future Messiah, second as the leader
of the repentant brothers, and third as an encouragement to all who have
greatly sinned and need to be forgiven.

Judah's repentance, like Joseph's willingness to trust, was a process.
The first signs of his change of heart were evident in Genesis 43, following

the return home after their first visit to Egypt. Aware that his father's reluctance to send Benjamin down to Egypt was jeopardising the survival of the whole starving family, he made the following striking offer:

> *'Send the boy along with me and we will go at once, so that we and you and our children may live and not die. I myself will guarantee his safety; you can hold me personally responsible for him. If I do not bring him back to you and set him here before you, I will bear the blame before you all my life. As it is, if we had not delayed, we could have gone and returned twice.'* (Gen. 43:8–10)

Here was a natural leader and persuasive communicator no longer using his gift to orchestrate destruction, but to bring salvation. Moreover, unlike Reuben before him who offered his sons as a guarantee, Judah was clearly taking *personal* responsibility. In effect, he was saying, if things don't work out, I alone will carry the can. The speech had its desired effect and the brothers, with Benjamin, returned for their second visit.

Yet Judah faced one final test, which finally demonstrated to Joseph (and God) that he was now a fully repentant and transformed character fit to be the forefather of who would be called the Lion of the tribe of Judah. Following their second visit, Benjamin was found to have Joseph's silver cup in his sack and was threatened with the prospect of being kept as a slave in Egypt. This led to Judah's finest hour. His moving speech, the longest in the whole of Genesis, included intercession and the offer of substitution.

His intercession was sincere, honouring to Joseph and heartfelt. Having given a full and honest account of the plight of the family, he came to the heart of his concern:

> *'So now, if the boy is not with us when I go back to your servant my father, and if my father, whose life is closely bound up with the boy's life, sees that the boy isn't there, he will die. Your servants will bring the grey head of our father down to the grave in sorrow.'* (Gen. 44:30–31)

The selfish, cruel, scheming, deceptive, immoral youth of chapters 37–38 had now become an unselfish, kind, candid, honest, upright man, no longer concerned first for his own wellbeing, but for that of his father. This intercession led, in turn, to the offer of substitution:

> 'Your servant guaranteed the boy's safety to my father. I said, "If I do not bring him back to you, I will bear the blame before you, my father, all my life!" Now then, please let your servant remain here as my lord's slave in place of the boy, and let the boy return with his brothers. How can I go back to my father if the boy is not with me? No! Do not let me see the misery that would come on my father.' (Gen. 44:32–34)

With this offer of self-sacrifice we see not only a beautiful picture of Jesus, but also of a now fully repentant sinner, ready to receive forgiveness and restoration both from God and from Joseph.

So what can we learn from Judah and the brothers? That sin has grievous consequences affecting God, others and ourselves. Yet, no matter how great our sin, there is a way back through repentance. This repentance is more than us being aware of our guilt, or fearful of the consequences of our actions, but rather involves a genuine transformation of heart in which we take full responsibility for what we have done. This doesn't mean that there is a guarantee that every person we have sinned against will necessarily forgive us or want to be reconciled with us, but it will ensure that we are forgiven and reconciled with the most important person of all, God Himself. And when we are right with Him, all things are possible.

Jacob: suffering because of the sin

It is important to realise that sin and relational breakdown often have consequences beyond those immediately involved. Very often there is a third party or persons who suffer greatly because of one man's sin against another. Sometimes those affected by strife are innocent bystanders caught in the fallout of other people's destructive actions. This was not, however, the case with Jacob.

Suffering he was; blameless he wasn't. As a father to his sons, by four different women, his parenting left a lot to be desired. Most notably it was his blatant favouritism of one of his sons that had led to the jealousy of the others. Moreover, 20 years on it was clear that he still hadn't learnt his lesson. Having charged his older sons to go down to Egypt he continued to show favouritism, refusing to send Benjamin with them:

> 'But Jacob did not send Benjamin, Joseph's brother, with the others, because he was afraid that harm might come to him. So Israel's sons were among those who went to buy grain, for the famine was in the land of Canaan also.' (Gen. 42:4–5)

Yet while acknowledging that Jacob was a prime cause for the troubles of the family, he was also a victim who suffered both openly at the 'loss' of his son and in ignorance at the 20-year deception by his other sons. The deep grief that he suffered was evident from the outset. On hearing the news of Joseph's 'death' we see how:

> 'Jacob tore his clothes, put on sackcloth and mourned for his son many days. All his sons and daughters came to comfort him, but he refused to be comforted. "No," he said, "I will continue to mourn until I join my son in the grave." So his father wept for him.' (Gen. 37:34–35)

Twenty years on, that grief still had a binding effect. It was partly fear of further loss that prevented him from releasing Benjamin for the first visit to Egypt. Later, the news that Simeon had been made a hostage to force Benjamin to go down to Egypt caused this heart-rending response:

> 'You have deprived me of my children. Joseph is no more and Simeon is no more, and now you want to take Benjamin. Everything is against me!' (Gen. 42:36)

This was pain upon pain and his response was to lash out at his sons. Maybe all along he had suspected them of having killed Joseph. The extent to which he seemed to resent the other brothers was highlighted in his response to Reuben's offer to guarantee Benjamin's safety:

> 'My son will not go down there with you; his brother is dead and he is the only one left. If harm comes to him on the journey you are taking, you will bring my grey head down to the grave in sorrow.' (Gen. 42:38)

Quite how Reuben and the other brothers must have felt, knowing that Benjamin seemed to be the only 'living' son that their father really cared for, can only be imagined.

More was to follow. With the famine getting worse, but trapped by Joseph's deal that they can only return with Benjamin, Jacob again lashed out at his sons:

> 'Why did you bring this trouble on me by telling the man you had another brother?' (Gen. 43:6)

Whether it was simply desperation at the situation, or the beginnings of a genuine change of heart, Jacob finally responded positively to Judah's offer to take personal responsibility for Benjamin's safety:

> 'Then their father Israel said to them, "If it must be, then do this: put some of the best products of the land in your bags and take them down to the man as a gift – a little balm and a little honey, some spices and myrrh, some pistachio nuts and almonds. Take double the amount of silver with you, for you must return the silver that was put back into the mouths of your sacks. Perhaps it was a mistake. Take your brother also and go back to the man at once. And may God Almighty grant you mercy before the man so that he will let your other brother and Benjamin come back with you. As for me, if I am bereaved, I am bereaved."' (Gen. 43:11–14)

Despite the begrudging and fatalistic tone of Jacob's response, the renewed use of the name 'God Almighty' (*El-Shaddai*) as the all-sufficient God is maybe expressive of the fact that somehow he knew God would make a way. The next time we hear about Jacob is as he receives the startling news that his favourite son Joseph is still alive (Gen. 45:25–28).

So what can we learn from Jacob's story here? First we need to realise, especially if we are in a position of authority, that our actions can have a great bearing on those we are called to care for. While there are no perfect parents or leaders, we must at all costs resist favouritism and lead with impartiality, and constantly seek God for help to be the best we possibly can be, and ask His forgiveness and grace for where we have fallen short. But there is a further lesson to us all. Sin has widespread consequences and many are the victims of family and relational strife. Children of divorced parents, for example, usually suffer deep grief and trauma that, outside of the grace of God, may never be healed. Church members who suffer from the effects of leadership fallout and church splits are all too common. That such damage can be done, but that such healing can come to so many, should be a further motivation (if we need any) to press through and seek full-scale relational reconciliation and restoration.

God: working to bring reconciliation

Jacob's action in releasing Benjamin and his acknowledgement of the need for the mercy of *El-Shaddai* was, in part, a recognition that there was a fourth and decisive player in this drama.

In his study, *Joseph: The Hidden Hand of God*, Liam Goligher emphasises God's sovereignty in the restoration of the family and poses the following important question:

> 'How far will God go to bring a family to himself? Apparently, he will go as far as it takes! In chapter 42 we find him working through an international crisis, through the administration and civil service of a

global power, and through his chosen man, Joseph ... setting the stage
for a rather bizarre family reunion. God uses Joseph to bring his family
to true repentance and then to save them from death by famine.'[11]

The providential God is working through circumstances and in human
hearts to bring about His sovereign purposes.

This is good news for all who are still suffering from family or
relationship breakdown. God is as committed to bringing reconciliation
now as He was then. While we must not wait to forgive, and while there
is no guarantee that reconciliation and subsequent restoration will always
take place in this life, we can be assured that God is working providentially
behind the scenes. If you have greatly sinned come to Him, confess your
sin and go before those you have offended. If you have been sinned
against, forgive, wait patiently and then slowly build trust. Whether now
or in eternity, we can be confident of this:

'we know that in all things God works for the good of those who love
him, who have been called according to his purpose.' (Rom. 8:28)

CHAPTER 9

GRACE REIGNS!

I want to tell you an encouraging story of reconciliation. It concerns a woman that I invited to Alpha a number of years ago. There, on that Alpha course, she experienced the greatest reconciliation of all – between her and her heavenly Father (2 Cor. 5:18–21). As a young Christian, she started growing enthusiastically in her faith, but was clearly struggling with her relationship with her stepfather and had not seen her natural father since she was three years old. But God is a God of reconciliation and restoration and He began to work on her behalf. On another discipleship course she felt prompted to write a letter to her biological father and having done so, immediately felt a sense of release. She then came to be ministered to over the issue of rejection and was able to forgive and let go of her unresolved anger towards her dad, resulting in 'the biggest release ever'. The following week was her birthday and, to her amazement, 'out of the blue' she received a letter from her long lost father. They corresponded and decided to meet up. I quote from her story:

> 'I went alone to meet him … he hugged me when he met me and it all felt right. I finally had a "dad's" hug … he told me that he loved me, he told me that he had always loved me.'

She then met up with her half-brother and sister, who explained that their dad had always acknowledged her in his heart, even though she didn't live with him. She continues:

> 'This was a great comfort to me. He had always cared – I just didn't know it. Then my half-sister explained about how guilty he felt. I said to her, "There's no need for guilt. It's in the past and that's where it should stay. We cannot change the past – the facts are there and no one can deny what happened. What is important now is the future and what we do with it." Five years on we are still talking, though not as much. I have met up with him on several occasions and he is my dad. I call him "Dad" and love him dearly. All feelings of rejection are gone

and I love the fact that God dealt with this and I have been able to move forward into the life he has destined for me!'

Since then she has continued to serve and be involved in her church as well as frequently ministering to the poor in Africa. She is beginning to live her dream.

Like this woman, forgiveness and relational reconciliation were a key part of Joseph's journey and may well be part of yours. Genesis 45, which tells of Joseph's reconciliation with his brothers, is rightly considered by many commentators as the climax of the whole narrative. If Genesis chapters 42–44 were about the two-year process of repentance and rebuilding trust, then chapter 45 is about the dramatic and moving high point when grace finally prevailed. Again, we have four key players: Joseph who is enabled to release grace, his brothers who receive grace, Jacob who is revived by grace, and God, ruling over all, through grace.

Joseph: releaser of grace

Whereas in Genesis 42–44 the brothers were the central characters, in Genesis 45 Joseph is once again the main player. As one who had been greatly sinned against, he now took the initiative and unconditionally released grace to his brothers. In doing so, he is a fitting example for all true followers of the living God. As Jesus Himself later stated:

> *'If another believer sins against you, go privately and point out the offense. If the other person listens and confesses it, you have won that person back.'* (Matt. 18:15, NLT)

Even without the guarantee of an easy journey or a positive response, Jesus makes clear that we, like Joseph, are to take the initiative in bringing reconciliation and release grace to those who have offended or sinned against us.

Yet, not only are we called to initiate reconciliation, we are called to do it well and wisely. Many a relationship has actually got worse through well-meaning but rash attempts at relational restoration. Once again, Joseph can teach us some important principles, the first of which is...

Be reconciled with the right people

This may seem a strange and unnecessary comment. After all, aren't we supposed to be reconciled with everyone? In an ideal world 'yes', but the fact is that we are not living in an ideal world. We are commanded to live at peace with all men where at all possible (Rom. 12:18). But the reality is that it is not always possible to do so. Interestingly, Jesus talks about initiating reconciliation with one who he terms your 'brother'. This may, as in Joseph's case, be literal family members, but in context it particularly applies to those who are part of the covenant family of God. Why is that so? Because if you try to be reconciled with someone you either don't know well, or who is not on the same spiritual wavelength, then an attempt to bring up past issues may make matters worse.

In Joseph's case there were a number of people who had offended him. There were the Ishmaelites who had sold him into slavery, Mrs Potiphar who had attempted to seduce him and then falsely slandered him, Potiphar who had chosen to believe his wife, and the cupbearer who had forgotten him. Yet we don't read of any attempt by Joseph to be reconciled with any of these. Why? It may simply be because these relationships were not central to the fulfilment of the dream or the providential purposes of God – the narrator is silent about how these relationships developed. But it may have been rather that none of these other characters were members of either Joseph's family or the covenant family of God, and that to have attempted reconciliation would not have achieved any positive end. Attempts at reconciliation with the Ishmaelite traders may have fallen on deaf ears. After all, they were just doing commercial business! To have revisited the false rape charge with Potiphar and his wife may well have been tempting – especially once Joseph came to power – but it is questionable whether it would have achieved any beneficial outcome. No, sometimes we just need to accept it is best to forgive others in the quietness of our hearts, trusting that God is just and that He will bring judgment and vindication, if not in this life, then in the next.

But with close family, friends, and those in the family of God it is a different matter. If Joseph had not been reconciled with his brothers and restored to his father, his life, blessed as it was, would still have been incomplete. Moreover, although Joseph would have been able to continue under God's gracious, prospering hand, the rest of the family would never have come into their destiny. The brothers would have stayed in guilt and fear all their lives, and would never have been able to be leaders of God's chosen people; and their names would never have appeared on the gates of the New Jerusalem (Rev. 21:12).

Initiating reconciliation with those in our family, friendship circle or the local church is vital and can potentially bring release and restoration to all concerned. Failing to be reconciled with these key people in our lives may hinder ours and their destiny in God. Yet, in seeking to bring swift resolution, we must also be careful to...

Be reconciled at the right time

This simply re-emphasises the lessons of the previous chapter. Joseph deliberately didn't press for reconciliation the moment he saw his brothers. Rather, he waited for two long years, probably in order see genuine repentance on the part of those who had offended him, until finally and dramatically he 'could no longer control himself' (Gen. 45:1).

What are we to make of this? If we are the one who has given the offence and we are aware that the other person has been offended then, as Jesus made clear in the Sermon on the Mount, we are to act swiftly:

> *'Therefore, if you are offering your gift at the altar and there remember that your brother has something against you, leave your gift there in front of the altar. First go and be reconciled to your brother; then come and offer your gift.'* (Matt. 5:23)

As an aside, this doesn't mean we should go up to people who are unaware of a problem and say, 'I need to ask you to forgive me because of my attitude towards you.' This may give them a problem that they didn't have!

When it comes to others having clearly offended us, as in the case of Joseph, then there is an important issue of timing. Sometimes, particularly when the issue is relatively minor, it is still best to seek reconciliation fairly quickly, rather than letting an issue fester. But when, for example, there is a more major offence and both parties are fully aware of what has happened, repentance on behalf of the one who has sinned is essential for full reconciliation to take place. Forgiveness can be instant, but the rebuilding of trust and therefore full reconciliation may need a process of time and the proof of genuine repentance.

Be reconciled in the right context

When the time is right it is vital that reconciliation is undertaken in the right context. Again, Joseph's example is instructive:

> 'Then Joseph could no longer control himself before all his attendants, and he cried out, "Make everyone leave my presence!" So there was no one with Joseph when he made himself known to his brothers.' (Gen. 45:1)

In others words, he made sure that he was not airing dirty linen in public. He gave the brothers the respect of hearing him out in private. He was not out to shame or embarrass them, so he chose a private forum.

He also did it face to face. He didn't try and do it through a third party. He, Joseph, spoke to them in person. This is almost always the best way to do things. Often, attempted reconciliation can go wrong when we violate these simple principles. How many situations have become worse because the communication was done impersonally? One of the worst ways to attempt to convey sensitive information to another person is via email. If the only way of making contact is via a letter, then make sure it is very carefully worded, both in content and tone. Better still is a phone call. But best of all by far is a carefully chosen, private, face-to-face environment. This, of course, is no guarantee of success. Vital to any healthy reconciliation is the need to...

Be reconciled with the right attitude

Attitude is all important! It is worth waiting until you have personally worked through to a place of total forgiveness *before* attempting reconciliation. We see glimpses of Joseph's mercy and heart to bless his brothers during the two-year testing, but it was at the point of revealing himself to them that it became apparent how completely free he was from bitterness and revenge. Instead, he was so overcome with emotion that his loud weeping was heard by the Egyptians. Moreover, his first words to his brothers were full of grace:

> *'Joseph said to his brothers, "I am Joseph! Is my father still living?"'*
> (Gen. 45:3)

First, he was simply concerned to make himself known to them, then he revealed what was most on his heart: the wellbeing of his father.

Faced with the terrified reaction of his brothers, Joseph continued graciously:

> *'"Come close to me." When they had done so, he said, "I am your brother Joseph, the one you sold into Egypt! And now, do not be distressed and do not be angry with yourselves for selling me here, because it was to save lives that God sent me ahead of you."'*
> (Gen. 45:4–5)

The call to come close was not a call to intimidate, but to show them that it was really him. Significantly, he didn't skirt around their offence; he called a spade a spade! But he stated their betrayal as a matter of fact and then immediately reassured them by highlighting the sovereignty of God in the whole matter. This was clearly not a man who was using the meeting as an attempt to get his own back or vent his anger, but one who had so thoroughly worked through the issues that he could talk about their offence secure in the knowledge that God had overruled all.

In addition, having brought his brothers face to face with himself, with their sin, and with God's sovereign grace, he immediately invited them to come and share in his blessing:

> 'Now hurry back to my father and say to him, "This is what your son Joseph says: God has made me lord of all Egypt. Come down to me; don't delay. You shall live in the region of Goshen and be near me – you, your children and grandchildren, your flocks and herds, and all you have. I will provide for you there"' (Gen. 45:9–11)

Again, his first concern was for his father and about his being restored to him, but this quickly moved on to a demonstration of grace and tenderness towards his brothers. He had clearly not only forgiven them, but had a genuine love and care for their wellbeing and protection, as expressed by his desire for them to live near him. In other words, he wanted them to be blessed! When you want to be close to those who have sinned against you and want to do good to them and see them prosper, it is a real indication that you have truly forgiven them. It is this attitude that is the key to true reconciliation.

Joseph was not just doing this out of legal duty. His heart had clearly been so softened that he was able to fully express his newfound love for them:

> 'Then he threw his arms around his brother Benjamin and wept, and Benjamin embraced him, weeping. And he kissed all his brothers and wept over them.' (Gen. 45:14–15)

This grace and forgiveness went much further than the erasing of the past. It included the promise of a great future. On hearing the news of this family reconciliation Pharaoh stepped in with a promise of extravagant generosity:

'Tell your brothers, "Do this: Load your animals and return to the
land of Canaan, and bring your father and your families back to me.
I will give you the best of the land of Egypt and you can enjoy the fat
of the land."' (Gen. 45:17–18)

This is clear evidence that God's promise to Abraham is still working. The covenant people are not only going into Egypt, but they are going to enjoy the best portion of the land. But it is also part of the broader picture of God's redemptive grace through Jesus Christ who now offers grace to all – unconditionally, tenderly, and with a view to us walking in all the blessings of the Father's house.

Finally, Joseph sent the brothers back, having loaded them with provisions and having given to each one a new set of clothing, before sending them away with the warning not to quarrel along the way. Once again we have a wonderful picture of the abundance of salvation. In Ephesians 1:3, for example, we are reminded that we have been 'blessed ... in the heavenly realms with every spiritual blessing in Christ.' But now that we are recipients of such grace and peace 'in Christ', and having been united together as one in Him, we must make every endeavour to keep that unity of the Spirit in the bond of peace (Eph. 4:1–6).

The brothers: recipients of grace

Unlike in Genesis 42–44 where the brothers are the main characters, Genesis 45 pictures them as stunned, largely passive recipients of grace. This is significant. The focal point of chapters 42–44 is their process of repentance; in chapter 45 the focus shifts to Joseph, the agent of reconciliation. Nevertheless, there are a number of lessons we can learn about their reaction.

First, their initial response was one of fear, maybe mixed with disbelief:

'his brothers were not able to answer him, because they were terrified at his presence.' (Gen. 45:3)

The parallel between their reaction and that of the early disciples after Jesus' resurrection seems particularly poignant. Mark describes the reactions of the women on seeing the tombstone rolled away, and having heard the strange news from the angel that Jesus who was crucified, had risen:

'Trembling and bewildered, the women went out and fled from the tomb. They said nothing to anyone, because they were afraid.' (Mark 16:8)

People react differently to the good news of Jesus and the opportunity to receive grace and reconciliation.

Undeterred by their hesitancy, Joseph spontaneously demonstrated his newfound love for them:

'And he kissed all his brothers and wept over them. Afterward his brothers talked with him.' (Gen. 45:15)

It was only after this demonstration of unconditional love and mercy that they began to be reassured. Like the prodigal son they were guilty and they knew it, but were clearly overwhelmed by passionate grace. Again, there is a clear parallel with the disciples after the resurrection:

'After his suffering, he presented himself to them and gave many convincing proofs that he was alive. He appeared to them over a period of forty days and spoke about the kingdom of God.' (Acts 1:3)

The brothers, recipients of the extravagant generosity of Joseph, then returned to Jacob to bring him back to the land of Goshen. By the time they greeted their father, they were fully convinced enough to tell him the good news:

'Joseph is still alive! In fact, he is ruler of all Egypt.' (Gen. 45:26)

So what can we learn from the brothers' response? That we cannot predict how people will respond to us if we initiate reconciliation – and there is no guarantee that it will always be positive. However, this must not stop us acting courageously and making the first move, following the wise example of Joseph and trusting in the working of a providential God. To those who will receive grace, their lives will be forever transformed.

Jacob: revived by grace

Jacob's reaction and subsequent restoration to his long lost son is one of the most moving passages in Scripture. Initially, he took some convincing:

> *'Jacob was stunned; he did not believe them. But when they told him everything Joseph had said to them, and when he saw the carts Joseph had sent to carry him back, the spirit of their father Jacob revived. And Israel said, "I'm convinced! My son Joseph is still alive. I will go and see him before I die."'* (Gen. 45:26–28)

This was a pivotal moment for this great patriarch. Up until this point he was still grieving and his faith was punctuated with moments of deep despair and fatalism. But on hearing the news that his favourite boy was still alive, his spirit was 'revived'. Moreover, as we shall see in the next chapter, this good news paved the way for Jacob to go down to Egypt. On the way, he had a fresh encounter with the Lord, had the joy of meeting Joseph, and safely saw his family settled in the land of Goshen.

Often there are those, like Jacob, who have suffered greatly because of the breakdown of relationships. Reconciliation between warring parties can have massive, positive repercussions, not just for those directly involved, but for those caught up in the battle. There are many innocent victims of injustice or conflict between others who, like Jacob, will be greatly 'revived', healed and restored as a result of true reconciliation by others.

God: the ruler of grace

The dramatic reconciliation between Joseph and his brothers, and the subsequent restoration of the family, was clearly brought about by the providence of God. Throughout, the writer wants us to see God as the hidden but central character of the whole Joseph story. He is clearly the source of Joseph's dreams, although not mentioned as such. He is specifically named as being with Joseph in slavery and in prison. He is given credit by Joseph for being the author and interpreter of the dreams of both Pharaoh and his two officials. He is honoured by Joseph for elevating him to ruler of Egypt, as seen in the naming of his two sons. Hence, Brueggemann is surely wrong in his assertion that until the reconciliation in chapter 45, 'We have not had a hint before now that Joseph had any notion of being a part of God's purpose'.[12]

Nevertheless, Joseph's speech in Genesis 45, where he openly acknowledges God's sovereignty throughout his entire journey, does seem to represent a stronger affirmation of divine providence than we have previously witnessed:

> 'it was to save lives that God sent me ahead of you ... God sent me ahead of you to preserve for you a remnant on earth and to save your lives by a great deliverance ... God has made me lord of all Egypt.'
> (Gen. 45:5,7,9)

The thrice repetition of 'God' makes clear who was ultimately in charge. To confidently state that God had sent him to Egypt is itself a remarkable statement. Here was a man who had suffered acutely, seemingly wasting his late teens and twenties in slavery and in prison, now declaring that ultimately God was using these events to fulfil His sovereign purposes.

Joseph had been lifted up, not for his own benefit, but to provide salvation and deliverance for the people of God.

This declaration of the sovereignty of God doesn't mean that somehow God is the author of sin and evil. Joseph twice made clear that the brothers were fully culpable for their actions:

> *'I am your brother Joseph, the one you sold into Egypt! And now, do not be distressed and do not be angry with yourselves for selling me here'* (Gen. 45:4–5)

Men are responsible for their deeds, yet God is clearly sovereign and in His sovereignty was willing and able to use the evil actions of men to fulfil His good purposes. Brueggemann, drawing on the words of Karl Barth that 'God accompanies the creature' forcefully makes this point:

> *'In Joseph's self-disclosure (vv5–8), we are at the centre of a great faith affirmation. Neither the freedom of the creature nor the gracious sovereignty of God is cancelled. They are not in conflict nor are they to be equated. God's will makes use of all human action but is domesticated or limited by no human choice.'*[13]

Such faith in the ultimate sovereignty of God over all things is integral to the theology of the whole Genesis narrative, and indeed to the rest of the Scriptures. Once again, the parallel with Jesus Christ is evident. He did suffer at the hands of His own people who, together with 'wicked men', killed Him. Yet this was all part of God's plan. He was 'sent ahead' to bring salvation and deliverance to both Jews and Gentiles and was raised from the dead to be Lord of heaven and earth. Peter makes this clear in his Pentecost sermon:

> *'This man was handed over to you by God's deliberate plan and foreknowledge; and you, with the help of wicked men, put him to death by nailing him to the cross. But God raised him from the dead,*

freeing him from the agony of death, because it was impossible for
death to keep its hold on him ... Therefore let all Israel be assured
of this: God has made this Jesus, whom you crucified, both Lord
and Messiah.' (Acts 2:23–24,36)

The good news is that this sovereign God has not only worked through
Joseph to provide salvation for the sons of Israel, He has also worked
through His Son, Jesus, to provide salvation for all mankind, Jew and
Gentile. We can now be reconciled with Him through Christ:

'All this is from God, who has reconciled us to himself through Christ
and gave us the ministry of reconciliation: that God was reconciling
the world to himself in Christ, not counting people's sins against them.
And he has committed to us the message of reconciliation. We are
therefore Christ's ambassadors, as though God were making his appeal
through us. We implore you on Christ's behalf: be reconciled to God.'
(2 Cor. 5:18–20)

Have you been reconciled with God? Are you at peace with God? If 'yes',
then rejoice! If 'no', then you can know this peace and healing by accepting
Jesus' sacrifice on your behalf and by believing that He is no longer counting
your sins against you, but will instead account Jesus' own righteousness to
you (2 Cor. 5:21).

Once reconciled with God, we must be reconciled with others. Flowing
from the ultimate act of reconciliation, now there is the possibility of full
reconciliation between nations, communities, families and individuals.
That is one of the central messages of the New Testament. In Ephesians,
for example, there is a strong emphasis on reconciliation between Jew and
Gentile. To Gentile believers, previously separated from God's covenants
and His people, there is great news:

'But now in Christ Jesus you who once were far away have been
brought near by the blood of Christ. For he himself is our peace,

who has made the two groups one and has destroyed the barrier, the dividing wall of hostility ... His purpose was to create in himself one new humanity out of the two, thus making peace' (Eph. 2:13–15)

Now that we are one in Christ we must:

'Make every effort to keep the unity of the Spirit through the bond of peace.' (Eph. 4:3)

Then we must endeavour to work out this unity not just within the Christian community, but also in the family and the marketplace (Eph. 5:21–6:9).

God is committed to relational reconciliation. Its benefits are immense and eternal: peace with Him and peace with others. Let's learn from the example of Joseph by shunning revenge and seeking reconciliation:

'If it is possible, as far as it depends on you, live at peace with everyone. Do not take revenge, my dear friends, but leave room for God's wrath, for it is written: "It is mine to avenge; I will repay," says the Lord. On the contrary: "If your enemy is hungry, feed him; if he is thirsty, give him something to drink. In doing this, you will heap burning coals on his head." Do not be overcome by evil, but overcome evil with good.' (Rom. 12:18–21)

These words would have been a fitting epitaph to the life of Joseph. Wherever possible, he sought to live at peace. He didn't seek revenge when offended, but left room for a sovereign God to move. He blessed his treacherous brothers and overwhelmed them with his generosity. Ultimately he triumphed. Rather than being overcome by evil, he overcame evil with good.

CHAPTER 10

SERVING THE FAMILY, SAVING THE WORLD

In his book, *From Success to Significance,* Lloyd Reeb addresses those who have achieved a measure of 'success' in their lives, but are at 'half-time' and are looking for something of greater 'significance' in the second half. He poses the question, what do you do when the pursuit of success isn't enough? Some look for a mid-life or end-of-life career change. Others simply broaden their horizon while continuing to operate successfully within their existing career path. Whatever path we choose, it is important that we determine to 'live beyond ourselves' and so make a lasting impact. This will inevitably involve not just looking after ourselves but serving others, helping them to reach their destiny.

Without suggesting that Joseph came to some mid-life crisis, there is evidence of a shift of focus as he entered the later years of his life. In worldly terms he had reached the pinnacle of influence and affluence at the relatively young age of 30. Moreover, his reconciliation with his brothers meant that the dreams of his youth had begun to be fulfilled before his very eyes. So the question is, what was left for him to do? The answer is found in Genesis 46–50 and is the subject of this penultimate chapter and the final one.

If the first part of Joseph's life was about him coming to a place of influence, the latter part was about him using that position to serve others. As we shall see from Genesis 46–47, Joseph's priority was first serving his father and family, and then serving Pharaoh and in turn saving the Egyptians from famine. This dual emphasis is important. Some Christians today so emphasise their outward call to mission and the marketplace that they neglect their inward ministry to their own families and fail to honour God's people in the gathered community of the Church. Others get stuck in navel-gazing, insular Christian groups, and fail to fulfil God's missional agenda. But we can learn from Joseph and become a truly 'both-and' people: first serving our families and God's family and then working together to serve and save the world around us.

Serving the family

Joseph's main focus in his later years was on serving his family. This was no ordinary family, but rather a special family, representing the people of God for all times and in all ages. As such, we can learn lessons about serving both our families and God's family, the Church.

Looking at Genesis as a whole we can see that Joseph's main historic role was to help save the people of Israel from the famine and provide them with a safe temporary homeland, before their exodus and return to the Promised Land. Although Joseph is a very significant character in his own right, as Stephen later depicted in Acts 7, he is essentially a transitional figure between Abraham and Moses.

There is a vital lesson for us to learn here. While each of us is uniquely loved and called by God, our individual role in life only ultimately makes sense in the context of the corporate destiny of the people of God. If we are to fulfil our full redemptive potential, we are called to be actively involved in seeing God's purposes established in and through His people. Yes, each of us has a vital part to play in the purposes of God in *our* generation, but we have generations before us and (if the Lord tarries) generations ahead of us. We must, therefore, honour and rejoice in our history in God.

The importance of this longer-term, intergenerational perspective is highlighted by the skilful interweaving of the stories of Jacob and Joseph throughout the second half of Genesis. Jacob is the main character of chapters 26–36, Joseph the hero of chapters 37–45, with a further shift back to Jacob from chapter 46 through to 50:14. This restoration of Jacob back to centre stage is particularly evident in Genesis 46–47: chapter 46 begins with him setting out to Egypt and then offering sacrifices at Beersheba; chapter 47 ends with him worshipping as he leaned. Joseph still has a vital role to play, but it is no longer about him achieving 'success', but about him attaining 'significance' through the service of his father and his family.

The reunion

In Genesis 46–47 we see Joseph serving his family. But first he was lovingly reunited with his father. Jacob's journey to Egypt is a stirring example to all 'fathers' in the faith. Now approaching 130, instead of contemplating retirement he became re-fired by the promise and purpose of God. Before leaving Canaan to go to Egypt he stopped at Beersheba, a significant place where both Abraham and Isaac had worshipped (21:33; 26:23–25). There he offered sacrifices to 'the God of his father Isaac'.

After years of apparent silence, God reappeared to Jacob in a night vision as 'God, the God of your father' (46:1–3). There God spoke to him reassuring him that although he was leaving the land, the promises both for descendants and for a return to the land were very much alive:

> 'Do not be afraid to go down to Egypt, for I will make you into a great nation there. I will go down to Egypt with you, and I will surely bring you back again. And Joseph's own hand will close your eyes.'
> (Gen. 46:3–4)

Energised by the promise, Jacob continued on his journey with all his family, including his grandchildren, his livestock and his possessions. What a grand procession they must have made! He was taking his future with him, a company of around seventy, representing the seedbed of the new nation. Like Jacob, we too must keep 'moving' in God, continually seeking Him and expecting Him to confirm that we are on track.

Having firmly re-established the story in the broader context of the story of the people of God, Joseph once again reappears and is reunited with his father. What is immediately obvious is the deep sense of love and affection between father and son:

'Joseph had his chariot made ready and went to Goshen to meet his father Israel. As soon as Joseph appeared before him, he threw his arms around his father and wept for a long time. Israel said to Joseph, "Now I am ready to die, since I have seen for myself that you are still alive."'
(Gen. 46:29–30)

One can only imagine the deep healing that took place for both father and son, highlighting our earlier lessons of the importance of relational reconciliation and full restoration wherever possible. Although Joseph was the high Egyptian official arriving in a chariot in the presence of his father, he was still the son, weeping in the embrace of his father. For us, too, where such reunions are possible, there is a powerful release of emotion that can have a major impact on our lives. This reunion was not only historically significant at the time, but it pointed the way to the future, to one greater than Joseph. To Jacob and his sons the appearance of Joseph, seemingly once dead but 'now alive', was a partial foreshadowing of the appearance of the resurrected Jesus to His disciples.

Moreover, as the living 'saviour' for his family, Joseph adopted the roles of intercessor and provider, pointing the way to Jesus Christ and to all believers who are now 'in Christ', called to intercede and provide for both their families and local churches.

Intercession

Joseph's 'intercession' before Pharaoh occupies a lengthy section at the close of chapter 46 and the beginning of chapter 47. It is the first and foremost way that he served his family:

'Then Joseph said to his brothers and to his father's household, "I will go up and speak to Pharaoh and will say to him, 'My brothers and my father's household, who were living in the land of Canaan, have come to me. The men are shepherds; they tend livestock, and they have brought along their flocks and herds and everything they own.' When Pharaoh calls you in and asks, 'What is your occupation?' you should answer,

'Your servants have tended livestock from our boyhood on, just as our
fathers did.' Then you will be allowed to settle in the region of Goshen,
for all shepherds are detestable to the Egyptians.'" (Gen. 46:31–34)

Leaving aside the discussion of whether Joseph was being devious, opportunistic or just prudent, the fact is that he is prepared to represent the brothers before Pharaoh, taking five of his brothers with him. The details here are important. It is the brothers, not Joseph, who have to make the actual request of Pharaoh: 'So now, please let your servants settle in Goshen' (Gen. 47:4). However, Pharaoh granted their request, not because of them but because of his relationship with Joseph who was standing there with them. Hence:

'Pharaoh said to Joseph, "Your father and brothers have come to you,
and the land of Egypt is before you; settle your father and your brothers
in the best part of the land. Let them live in Goshen. And if you know
of any among them with any special ability, put them in charge of my
own livestock."' (Gen. 47:5–6)

So, what if anything can we learn from this passage about intercession? While Joseph is not Jesus and Pharaoh is not God (even if he thought he was!), nevertheless the parallels between Joseph's intercession before Pharaoh and Jesus' intercession before the Father are too important to miss. One of the best definitions of intercession is found in Ezekiel 22:30:

'I looked for someone among them who would build up the wall and
stand before me in the gap on behalf of the land so that I would not
have to destroy it, but I found no one.'

Thankfully, Jesus, the Son of God and the only totally righteous man who ever lived, stood in the gap for us through His work on the cross. Now alive and at the right hand of the Father, He 'always lives to intercede' for us (Heb. 7:25). But what does that mean? Some have mistakenly interpreted this to mean that Jesus is 'praying' for us. But it is more accurate to say that He is representing us before the Father on the basis of His finished work of intercession. Liam Goligher highlights Jesus' role as our great High Priest and our only mediator: 'He opens the way, smooths the path and acts as guarantor for sinners approaching God'.[14]

In that sense He is the only true intercessor or mediator between God and man (1 Tim. 2:5). If we look at Joseph, a similar point is made. It is because he represents the brothers to Pharaoh that the brothers receive a favourable response.

So what role, if any, do we play? The answer is a vital one! On the basis of Jesus' work of intercession on our behalf we are called to pray prayers of intercession. This is borne out in the telling words of Jesus Himself:

> '*Until now you have not asked for anything in my name. Ask and you will receive, and your joy will be complete ... In that day you will ask in my name. I am not saying that I will ask the Father on your behalf.*'
> (John 16:24,26)

What could be clearer? Jesus is not praying, but rather (like Joseph) He is interceding or representing us. We (like the brothers) are to do the actual praying, asking the Father in Jesus' name. We can and should of course pray for ourselves, but we are also called to pray for our families and for His family – the Church. As a husband and father, for years I have sought to pray for the wellbeing and salvation of my family. As a church leader I regularly pray for the local church. As a believer I am called to pray for all the saints:

> '*And pray in the Spirit on all occasions with all kinds of prayers and requests. With this in mind, be alert and always keep on praying for all the Lord's people [the saints].*' (Eph. 6:18)

Can I encourage you to pray daily and fervently for those in your world? Why not pray, 'Your kingdom come, Your will be done' over your family, your friends, your church and then over your unsaved friends, work colleagues and neighbours? Pray to the Father, with the help of the Spirit on earth and Jesus in heaven.

Provision

Having interceded before Pharaoh and received a favourable response, Joseph then ensured that his family was properly provided for:

'So Joseph settled his father and his brothers in Egypt and gave them property in the best part of the land, the district of Rameses, as Pharaoh directed. Joseph also provided his father and his brothers and all his father's household with food, according to the number of their children.' (Gen. 47:11–12)

The transformation was remarkable. Instead of starving in Canaan the family were now settled in the fertile land of Goshen where they could prosper physically and spiritually:

'Now the Israelites settled in Egypt in the region of Goshen. They acquired property there and were fruitful and increased greatly in number.' (Gen. 47:27)

Joseph indeed provided for his family well and is a great example to us today in giving of his time, talents and treasure.

First, he gave his time. Despite his important role as second-in-command to Pharaoh, Joseph was not too busy in his job to minister to the needs of his family. He took time out to go to Goshen and welcome his father. He made time to intercede before Pharaoh on behalf of his family and then to ensure that they were properly settled in Goshen. In the same way we must make sure that we don't so overwork that we cannot give quality time to serving our family and our church.

Second, Joseph gave of his talents. He did not keep his considerable gifts and huge influence just for serving Pharaoh, but he used his position to serve his family. This is a great reminder to those who God has blessed with significant marketplace ministries to not just use those talents to serve 'in the world', but to offer those same gifts to serve in and through the Church and so help fulfil God's mission to the ends of the earth.

Third, Joseph gave of his treasure or, more accurately, of the treasure of Pharaoh! He was not ashamed to use the huge wealth that was at his disposal to ensure that his own family was well cared for. This is important for us to grasp today. As the apostle Paul makes clear, we have a financial responsibility towards our families:

> 'Anyone who does not provide for their relatives, and especially for their own household, has denied the faith and is worse than an unbeliever.'
> (1 Tim. 5:8)

This is strong language and highlights how we as believers are to especially care for close family.

Moreover, throughout the Scriptures, there is an even clearer call for us to look after God's house. A few examples will suffice. In Haggai, for example, the Lord rebukes His people for leaving His house in ruins, 'while each of you is busy with your own house' (Hag. 1:9). Moreover, in the well-known passage in Malachi, the Lord reprimanded the people for 'robbing' Him by not bringing in the appropriate tithes and offerings. They are urged to rectify the situation, with corresponding promises of blessings if they are obedient:

> '"Bring the whole tithe into the storehouse, that there may be food in my house. Test me in this," says the LORD Almighty, "and see if I will not throw open the floodgates of heaven and pour out so much blessing that there will not be room enough to store."' (Mal. 3:10)

It is clear from the New Testament that God's house is no longer a physical house but a spiritual one, 'which is the church of the living God, the pillar and foundation of the truth' (1 Tim. 3:15). As Christians today we have a responsibility to financially invest in God's house, the local church.

So how did Joseph provide for his family? In the best possible way! The provision of the land of Goshen for the people of Israel was important both for their future economic and spiritual survival. Not only was it the 'best' part of the land, but it was separate, thus enabling the Israelites to prosper, grow and multiply in a pagan land without fully imbibing the culture and worship of that land. As we see from their future wilderness experience, most notably in the building of the golden calf, this 'separation' was only partially successful. Nevertheless, after more than four hundred years in a foreign land, the nation had been able to grow from one family to a nation of several million with its own distinct culture, still united in their sense of identity as the people of Yahweh.

This is important for us today. On the one hand we must realise that we are not called to *physical* separation as the children of Israel were. On the other hand we are called to radical *spiritual* separation. We are now seated with Christ in heavenly places and blessed with every spiritual blessing (Eph. 1:3; 2:6–7). The New Testament makes quite clear that spiritually we are called to 'come out' and 'be separate' (2 Cor. 6:17). Our Goshen is a land of being in and living in Christ, freed from the slavery and compromise of the worship of the world around us. But this doesn't mean that we are to be removed from the world and therefore unable to influence it. Quite the opposite! Although not of the world we are clearly called to be in it. In fact, we are called to live as salt and light and to be missionaries of the kingdom of God in the world in which we live.

Saving the world

This calling to kingdom influence in the world is clearly seen in the way that Joseph interacts with Pharaoh and the people of Egypt. Genesis 46–47 provides us with some great lessons as to how we are to impact the pagan world around us especially concerning how to honour earthly authorities and minister in the marketplace.

Honouring earthly authorities

We have already briefly looked at Joseph's relationship with Pharaoh as an example of intercession. But there is a further lesson for us, which is the importance of continuing to honour earthly authorities. First, Joseph himself clearly understood that Pharaoh was his boss and that if he wanted favour for his family he needed to approach Pharaoh correctly. He didn't attempt to bypass Pharaoh, but instead encouraged the brothers to approach the king directly. Unsurprisingly, given the history of relationship between Joseph and Pharaoh, Pharaoh granted great favour to the family. Having received what he wanted for his family, Joseph didn't stop there, but went on to introduce his father to Pharaoh. There then followed a poignant interchange in which the 130-year-old patriarch twice blessed the powerful Pharaoh:

'*Jacob blessed Pharaoh ... Then Jacob blessed Pharaoh and went out from his presence.*' (Gen. 47:7,10)

That Jacob blessed Pharaoh, not the other way around, is significant. Egypt needed the blessing of the people of the promise. Commentators highlight the importance of this event. Claus Westermann writes, 'The solemnity of this blessing is evident: Jacob, an alien shepherd from the steppes, who must ask Pharaoh for bread, appears before the powerful king of a mighty empire – and blesses him'[15]

This relationship clearly benefitted both parties. As Gordon Wenham expresses:

'*Because the Pharaoh has acknowledged Jacob's special status by receiving him graciously and honouring his sons, he and his countrymen may expect to find blessing through Jacob and his descendants ... The most immediate fulfilment of this blessing is Joseph's rescue of Egypt from the effects of famine.*'[16]

Such a positive relationship between the Church and civil authorities is an important aspect of kingdom life today. We have certainly seen this in our history as a church here in Peterborough. From 2001, we strongly sensed the Lord calling us to 'buy land' and start building. Having begun to outgrow the largest rented facility available in the city (eventually meeting there in three services), we felt compelled to go and look for a site to buy and build on. We eventually identified a particular site and drew up plans for a building. After considerable time and expense we submitted our planning application only to be turned down on a 4–3 vote. Coming out of that meeting somewhat shocked and disappointed, we quickly recognised that the way we responded to this seeming setback would be vital to our future progress. So, sensing somehow that the Lord was overruling, we determined not to allow a negative attitude to develop towards the City Council, pointedly telling the congregation that we were going to continue to honour those in authority. Later, having decided to let that site go, we were drawn to a far better site, double the size of the original and superior in every way. Through a series of circumstances I managed to get a meeting with the chief executive of the City Council, who caught the vision for what we were trying to do and saw that our building would be good for the city. So, we went back to planning, supported by the City Council and with letters of support from both the resident Labour MP and the Conservative candidate. This time we won the vote 9–0!

Now, with a stunning facility, we have not only seen great growth in the local church, but we have also been more able to serve the city. The blessing is mutual and we believe that we are moving towards fulfilling our missional mandate. Honouring authorities is vital if we want to walk in the favour of God!

Ministry in the marketplace

However, not only does Joseph show us the importance of honouring authorities, he also sheds light on the important question of ministering in the marketplace. First, we need to make clear that there is a huge cultural difference between Joseph's administration of Egypt during the famine and working as a business leader in one of today's modern capitalist economies, and we must be careful not to make over-simplistic connections between the two. It is also important to note that the narrator is largely describing events rather than commenting on them and is not, therefore, necessarily giving approval to all of Joseph's actions.

However, the overall tone of the narrative is that Joseph ruled Egypt during the famine in an exemplary fashion. As he had done earlier with Potiphar and the prison warder, he is depicted as continuing on from his diligent oversight in Genesis 41. On Pharaoh's behalf he received money (47:14–15), livestock (47:16–17), land (47:20) and slaves (47:21) from the people of Egypt. As Lindsay Wilson has commented:

> 'Joseph has engineered a scenario in which he is able to secure for Pharaoh control over the land and its people, perhaps regaining them from the Egyptian nobility. The task of a courtier is to advance the interests of his master and Joseph has certainly accomplished that. This is especially important when, as here, the survival of the people was at stake.'[17]

This highlights lessons that we learned in Chapters 5 and 6 of this study concerning the importance of diligently serving earthly bosses. Joseph is clearly being commended for his creative, diligent and effective leadership of Egypt in a way that benefits his master. As such he can be rightly used as an example to us all of the importance of marketplace ministry and an encouragement to be the best we can in whatever situation we are placed, knowing that it is ultimately Christ Himself who we are serving.

But what are we to make of the consequences of Joseph's administration with the Egyptians becoming slaves to Pharaoh? This is unsurprisingly one of the most controversial passages of the whole Joseph story. Is this a potential blot on his character? Brueggemann certainly thinks so:

> 'As though to set the stage for the Exodus, the result of Joseph's tax reform is that citizens sell their person to the throne ... They become bond servants and forfeit their freedom. Joseph may be credited with shrewdness. But for a tradition looking to the Exodus, it is a doubtful credit.'[18]

In other words, with the hindsight of Exodus when the Jews themselves became slaves, the fact that Joseph allowed the Egyptians to become slaves under his leadership is a dubious legacy. At first glance Brueggemann seems to have a point. However, a closer look at the text itself suggests a different conclusion, with the Egyptians themselves seeming to be grateful to Joseph and crediting him with saving their lives (Gen. 47:25). So, how are we to understand this? Another leading commentator very helpfully points out that slavery would have been viewed very differently to them then than to us now. Wenham writes:

> 'Memories of the African slave trade colour our view of slavery, so that
> we cannot understand this expression of gratitude. But in ancient
> society slavery was the accepted way of bailing out the destitute, and
> under a benevolent master could be quite a comfortable status ...
> Indeed, the law envisages some temporary slaves electing to become
> permanent slaves rather than take the freedom to which they were
> entitled after six years of service. Ancient slavery at its best was like
> tenured employment, whereas the free man was more like someone
> who was self-employed. The latter may be freer, but he faces more risks
> (Exod. 21:5–6; Deut. 15:12–17).'[19]

In other words, the Egyptians would have seen Joseph's actions as a blessing, not as a curse.

Certainly the overall impression we get from the passage as a whole is that the narrator is presenting Joseph's actions in a largely positive light. First, there is a link with other parts of the story. Genesis 47 is clearly seen as a continuation of Joseph's administration of the famine in chapter 41, where his role is presented very positively. Moreover, having just provided for his family, which of course is a good thing, the implication is that providing for the 'world' too is also a good thing.

There are a number of other specific factors that suggest we are to view Joseph not just as a shrewd but also a merciful administrator. Of particular importance is the fact that it is the Egyptians themselves who took the initiative in offering their lives in slavery, as opposed to Joseph imposing this on them. In the light of the earlier comments concerning the more positive view of slavery in that culture, it is surely significant that Joseph's offer of 80% of the crops in return for slavery is seen as a generous action. Rather than seeing, as Brueggemann does, an unfavourable link to the Israelites' slavery in Egypt, it is more likely that we are to view Joseph's actions as *contrasting* that of the later Pharaoh. Instead of the forced oppression, hard labour and deliberately vindictive 'bricks without straw' (Exod. 1;5), here we have the Egyptians willingly offering themselves and Joseph refusing to exploit them harshly. In Exodus, the Israelites unquestionably viewed Pharaoh as a cruel oppressor; in Genesis, the Egyptians praised Joseph as their saviour: 'You have saved our lives.'

Without undermining this emphasis on Joseph's merciful leadership of Egypt, some commentators highlight the *contrast* between the children of Israel prospering as free people in the land of Goshen with the Egyptians surviving through slavery (such as Bruce Waltke[20]). Liam Goligher takes this a step further, emphasising that the relevant point is that: 'Joseph rules Egypt for the benefit of the people of God, just as Christ rules in heaven for the benefit of his elect'.[21] Yet, while God is concerned with saving His people, Israel, we must not neglect the fact that Joseph (and God through him), does save the lives of the Egyptians, too.

This highlights how vital it is that we don't just focus on God's plan for the Church, but for the world at large. In recent decades throughout the Western world, many leaders have been sensing a growing responsibility to start tackling some of the critical issues of our day, such as human trafficking and child poverty. Well-known business leaders like Warren Buffet, for example, have decided to invest billions of their wealth into helping the Developing World through the Bill Gates Foundation. The same is happening throughout the body of Christ. Church leaders, churches and multitudes of believers are increasingly aware of their responsibility and that God's mission in the world includes getting involved with very practical, social needs.

Will you join the growing army of those who want to make a difference to the world today?

What conclusions can we draw from Joseph's work in Egypt for our own ministry and mission in the world? The first is that we are clearly called to honour earthly authorities, whether they share our faith or not. The second follows on from this: we must work hard in serving our employers and, where possible, view making money in a positive light. Third, wherever possible, marketplace ministry must have a higher goal than just economic prosperity, but must result in helping to alleviate injustice and poverty. Joseph helped save the physical lives of both Israel and Egypt. We are called to offer not only physical, but also spiritual salvation through Jesus Christ to all.

CHAPTER 11

FINISHING WELL

It's not just how you start, it's how you finish that matters. This principle applies in every sphere, from sports, to painting a picture, to marriage, to raising your children, to building a great ministry or indeed to running the race of life. Many start well, sprinting out of the blocks, only to fade before the finish line. History, including biblical history, is littered with 'greats' who ended up messing up. The two colossi of the Old Testament, Moses and David, both ended their lives less than gloriously and Solomon's later life was wrecked by turning away from the Lord, with all the tragic consequences that ensued in subsequent generations.

But Joseph stands out as a man who finished well. Suddenly promoted at the age of 30, he persevered and remained at the top for the next 80 years. Notably absent from his later years were any spiritual, moral, sexual or financial scandals. Instead, he died in good standing with his family, his boss, his adopted nation and his God. As such he provides us today with a marvellous example of how to finish well and illustrates, in particular, the importance of leaving a godly legacy, honouring key relationships and having faith for the future. Let's look at each of these in turn...

Leaving a godly legacy

The issue of legacy is huge! Apart from the relatively few who live a largely isolated life and leave no legacy, most of us will leave a legacy of some sort or other. The question is, will it be bad, good or great? This applies whether we have children or not. Obviously, the most direct impact we are likely to have will be on our natural or adopted children and through them to subsequent generations. One of the finest legacies is that of the eighteenth-century revivalist Jonathan Edwards and his godly wife, Sarah. From their eleven children came 1,400 descendants who included:

- 13 college presidents
- 65 professors
- 100 lawyers and a dean of a law school

- 30 judges
- 66 physicians
- 80 public office holders, including:
  - three mayors
  - three governors
  - three US senators
  - one controller of the US treasury
  - one vice-president of the US Government

This may be a hard act to follow, but we all can leave a good legacy. Even if we don't have children we still have a vital role to play in positively investing in others within the family of God, thereby faithfully passing on the baton of God's purposes to the next generation.

In Joseph's case, he was able to leave a great legacy for his sons. Critical to this was his positive relationship with his father and the blessing that he himself received from him. The story is told in Genesis 48–49 of Jacob first blessing Joseph's sons and then his own sons. Jacob is the prime mover, with Joseph playing a largely subordinate and submissive role. Yet, as a result, Joseph receives a great blessing and is able to pass on a great legacy to his descendants.

First, Joseph secured a blessing for his sons:

> *'Some time later Joseph was told, "Your father is ill." So, he took his two sons Manasseh and Ephraim with him.'* (Gen. 48:1)

Jacob responded by adopting Joseph's sons as his own, before bestowing a prophetic blessing on both, deliberately giving the blessing of the firstborn to the younger son, Ephraim. Jacob is clearly the initiator and Joseph largely passive, first protesting and then submitting to his father's decree. In so doing we are left in no doubt that he thereby submitted to God's sovereign will. In the words of Brueggemann:

'We are not dealing with the capriciousness or carelessness of an old man. Rather, we are faced with the hidden power of God, who reshapes history'[22]

Second, Joseph received his own blessing from Jacob. Genesis 49 is taken up with Jacob pronouncing 'blessing' on each one of his sons. Some of these, notably in the case of Reuben, were far from positive, whereas, unsurprisingly, Joseph received the longest and, apart from Judah, the most significant inheritance of all. Here, Jacob looks back and summarises highlights of Joseph's life as well as looking forward in prophetic blessing:

'Joseph is a fruitful vine, a fruitful vine near a spring, whose branches climb over a wall. With bitterness archers attacked him; they shot at him with hostility. But his bow remained steady, his strong arms stayed supple, because of the hand of the Mighty One of Jacob, because of the Shepherd, the Rock of Israel, because of your father's God, who helps you, because of the Almighty, who blesses you with blessings of the skies above, blessings of the deep springs below, blessings of the breast and womb. Your father's blessings are greater than the blessings of the ancient mountains, than the bounty of the age-old hills. Let all these rest on the head of Joseph, on the brow of the prince among his brothers.' (Gen. 49:22–26)

The result of these blessings over Joseph and his sons was a truly great inheritance. When Joshua allotted the land to the tribes, having first given Judah the largest share in the south, he then gave priority to Ephraim and Manasseh, Joseph's descendants. Ephraim and the half tribe of Manasseh were given the most fertile and largest portion of the land of Canaan (with the other half tribe of Manasseh receiving an inheritance east of the Jordan). Having initially only been given one portion of land, Joshua decided that the tribes of Joseph were so numerous that they needed a double portion:

'Then Joshua said to the tribes of Ephraim and Manasseh, the descendants of Joseph, "Since you are so large and strong, you will be given more than one portion."' (Josh. 17:17, NLT)

So the prophecy of Jacob was fulfilled and the blessing on Joseph's descendants was confirmed.

More than that, not only did Joseph receive and pass on a large and blessed legacy for the two tribes of his sons, he was also the forefather of some of Israel's greatest leaders: most notably, Joshua himself, three of the Judges – Gideon, Jephthah and Deborah – plus the great prophet, Samuel. A great leader was the ancestor of future great leaders in the generations to come.

I don't know about you, but this inspires me to live beyond myself and to look beyond this life to leaving a great future legacy. In fact, this issue of legacy usually becomes increasingly important to those who genuinely re-assess their lives at 'half-time'. I referred in the previous chapter to Lloyd Reeb's *From Success to Significance*. His testimony of the way he set a new course for the second half of his life is worth quoting in full:

'I didn't sell my business or quit my job. Instead, I redefined success, re-allocated my energies and re-prioritised my family's spending. I cut the time I spent doing business, found a niche as one of the pastors at a large church in Charlotte, North Carolina, and helped high-capacity people find their second-half calling. As a result, my wife, Linda, and I have had more time over the past decade to spend with our three kids as they grow, time to spend together playing tennis and sailing. I have enjoyed getting back into good physical shape and building a few close friendships. By allocating part of my week to ministry, I've had the thrill of being part of many men's and women's spiritual journeys as they pursue God and explore their personal faith, and I have travelled around the world on mission trips. I feel blessed to have had the freedom to invest a good part of my life in things that I believe have eternal significance.'[23]

Like Joseph, Lloyd had clearly become more concerned about long-term legacy than short-term success. You and I can make similar adjustments. Whether you are a young person or are at mid-life or in your later years, regardless of your social or financial position, you can begin to re-prioritise and start building for eternity rather than just the here and now.

An essential part of this re-prioritisation will be to invest more time and energy in family and other key relationships.

Honouring key relationships

Relationships often become more important as life goes on. This is not just for the multitudes of besotted grandparents, but for many who come to realise that 'success' needs to be redefined in relational terms. Certainly this was something that Joseph seemed to have grasped in his later years. If chapters 48–49 were focused on the issue of generational blessing, the final chapter of Genesis is all about Joseph's relationships, providing us with a cameo of his faithful dealings with his father, with Pharaoh, with his brothers and with his sons and grandsons.

Joseph and his father

Joseph's relationship with his father is of utmost importance throughout the narrative. This is particularly evident in the events surrounding Jacob's death. Joseph's response to the news that his father had died, was characteristically filled with emotion: 'Joseph threw himself on his father and wept over him and kissed him' (Gen. 50:1). Having already been charged by his father to ensure that he would be buried with his forefathers in Canaan (see chapter 47), Joseph proceeded to carry out this instruction with great diligence. First, he had the morticians embalm the body – a process lasting 40 days – then he led a 70-day period of national mourning, during which time he secured Pharaoh's permission to bury his father in the land of Canaan, taking a huge entourage with him including all the senior officers of Egypt and the entire household of Jacob. Having arrived in Canaan he then held a seven-day period of mourning before taking Jacob's body to the cave of Machpelah and burying him there.

Reading this account, one cannot fail to be impressed with the love and honour that Joseph gave to his deceased father. Loved and favoured by his father as a boy, cruelly separated, but now reconciled, Joseph had the privilege of fulfilling his father's wishes. I have sometimes witnessed firsthand the way that a number of the team here at KingsGate have cared for their elderly relatives. Whether in sickness or in health, I have been impressed by the love, care and provision shown often right through until death, and I intend to learn from theirs and Joseph's godly example.

Joseph and Pharaoh

The burial in Canaan was only possible because Joseph was still very much in good standing with the other key authority figure in his life, the Egyptian Pharaoh. Joseph had first come before Pharaoh as a young Hebrew slave. Now, decades later, he still ruled Egypt on Pharaoh's behalf with this remarkable alliance very much intact. Much of this was undoubtedly due to Joseph's wisdom and grace in dealing with his powerful boss. Rather than act in an underhand or independent way, he humbly but confidently appealed to Pharaoh for a leave of absence:

> *'Joseph said to Pharaoh's court, "If I have found favour in your eyes, speak to Pharaoh for me. Tell him, 'My Father made me swear an oath and said, "I am about to die; bury me in the tomb I dug for myself in the land of Canaan." Now let me go up and bury my father; then I will return.'"'* (Gen. 50:4–5)

It is an indication of the high regard with which Pharaoh held Joseph that he immediately agreed to his request, sending with him a great number of his counsellors and advisers, all the senior officers of Egypt and a great number of chariots. This was someone who clearly enjoyed the complete trust of his boss.

The strength of this relationship seems to have endured not only during the remainder of Joseph's lifetime, but also for some time afterwards. The writer of the Exodus describes the later oppression of the Israelites in Egypt as taking place only when a new king came to the throne who did not know about Joseph (Exod. 1:8). Joseph's reputation was obviously such that he was held in high standing with Pharaoh, sufficient to ensure the blessing and protection of his fellow Hebrews.

Joseph and his brothers

Not only did Joseph manage to maintain a great relationship with both his father and Pharaoh, but he also died with his relationship with his brothers fully restored. This in itself is remarkable, given the huge betrayal and injustice that Joseph had earlier suffered at their hands. It is also a sign that Joseph understood the principle of total forgiveness. A couple of incidents at the close of his life demonstrated the sincerity and completeness of his grace towards them.

The first concerned the burial of his father. Although Joseph used his position of authority to take the lead in enabling the burial of his father in Canaan, he made no attempt to exclude the brothers from being able to honour their father too. Rather, the narrator highlights that Joseph also took his brothers and the entire household of Jacob to Canaan (Gen. 50:8). Moreover, having together observed a seven-day period of mourning, Joseph and his brothers are clearly depicted as being united in carrying out their father's wishes:

> 'So Jacob's sons did as he had commanded them: they carried him to the land of Canaan and buried him ... After burying his father, Joseph returned to Egypt, together with his brothers' (Gen. 50:12–14)

The second incident took place following the funeral, with the brothers understandably nervous at how Joseph would treat them now that their father was gone:

*'When Joseph's brothers saw that their father was dead, they said,
"What if Joseph holds a grudge against us and pays us back for all
the wrongs we did to him?" So they sent word to Joseph, saying,
"Your father left these instructions before he died: 'This is what you
are to say to Joseph: I ask you to forgive your brothers the sins and the
wrongs they committed in treating you so badly.' Now please forgive the
servants of the God of your father."'* (Gen. 50:15–17)

Whether they were accurately representing their father's instructions or
not, their apprehension is clear. Yet they need not have feared. Joseph's
first response was to break down and weep. When his brothers came to
him, bowed low to him, and said 'we are your slaves', Joseph responded
in a way that was clearly contrary to their expectations:

*'But Joseph said to them, "Don't be afraid. Am I in the place of God?
You intended to harm me, but God intended it for good to accomplish
what is now being done, the saving of many lives. So then, don't be
afraid. I will provide for you and your children." And he reassured
them and spoke kindly to them.'* (Gen. 50:19–21)

This response sheds more light on the character of the mature Joseph
and is one of the most striking pictures of faith towards God and
forgiveness towards others found in the whole Bible. First, Joseph
displayed a genuine humility and faith in the sovereignty of God.
He had a healthy fear of the Lord that prevented him from attempting
to take God's place as judge and exact revenge. Second, his perspective
on his troubles is highly instructive. Without attributing his suffering
to God, he clearly saw the hand of God in his elevation and understood,
in a way that he could not have done when he first had his dreams, that
he had been unusually favoured and elevated to a high position not for
his own aggrandisement but in order to save many lives. In the words
of Brueggemann commenting on Genesis 50:20:

'we do not have simply a climax to the story. We have a programmatic
affirmation of the gospel which has governed the entire story. The evil
plans of human folks do not defeat God's purpose. Instead, they
unwittingly become ways in which God's plan is furthered'[24]

Secure in God's purpose, Joseph was therefore able to freely and willingly extend grace to his brothers. Without denying that they had meant him 'evil' he didn't use this opportunity to scold them or remind them of their guilt. Rather, he twice told them not to be afraid and spoke kindly to them, reassuring them. Neither was he content to merely forgive them for their offence, he went on to promise to take care of them and their families. How like Jesus, who not only forgives us our offences, but gives us His righteousness and makes us co-heirs with Himself.

Unsurprisingly, this remarkable display of generosity ensured that Joseph's last days were seemingly lived out in complete harmony with his brothers (Gen. 50:22). In this context, Joseph demonstrated the full extent of his grace towards them by entrusting them with the precious task of taking his bones to their future homeland: clearly a sign that the trust, once so badly violated, had been fully restored.

This brings the Joseph story full circle. The brothers who hated him are now living in harmony with him. All the lessons that we have learned throughout on the importance of walking in forgiveness and pressing through to relational reconciliation reach their conclusion here.

Joseph and his sons and grandsons

The final, and arguably the greatest, relational blessing of Joseph's final years was that he was able to enjoy being a father, grandfather, great-grandfather and even a great-great grandfather. In a telling conclusion, we see:

'Joseph lived to the age of 110. He lived to see three generations of
descendants of his son Ephraim, and he lived to see the birth of the
children of Manasseh's son Makir, whom he claimed as his own.'
(Gen. 50:22–23, NLT)

Joseph was clearly enjoying the blessing of long life, as emphasised by the thrice repetition of the word 'lived'. In particular, he was given the privilege of seeing three generations of his son Ephraim.

This highlights that at the end of one's life, what really matters are one's closest relationships. It is indeed true that no man on his death bed ever said, 'I wish I had spent more time in the office!'

Faith for the future

As wonderful as the example of Joseph is to us, both throughout his life and towards the end of his life, there is one final detail of Joseph's life that is arguably the most remarkable of all: his faith for his future beyond the grave. It is this that, hundreds of years later, the writer of the Hebrews chose to highlight:

> *'It was by faith that Joseph, when he was about to die, said confidently that the people of Israel would leave Egypt. He even commanded them to take his bones with them when they left.'* (Heb. 11:22, NLT)

Apparently greater than his dreams, his ability to forgive, his strength against sexual temptation, his patience in prison, his interpretation of dreams, his rule over Egypt, his reconciliation with his brothers, his serving of his family and his saving of Egypt, was Joseph's faith for the future of his bones! So striking is the selection of this fact in the great 'faith chapter' of Hebrews 11 that it is worth studying the fuller Genesis account in more detail:

> *'"Soon I will die," Joseph told his brothers, "but God will surely come to help you and lead you out of this land of Egypt. He will bring you back to the land he solemnly promised to give to Abraham, to Isaac, and to Jacob." Then Joseph made the sons of Israel swear an oath, and he said, "When God comes to help you and lead you back, you must take*

my bones with you." So Joseph died at the age of 110. The Egyptians
embalmed him, and his body was placed in a coffin in Egypt.'
(Gen. 50:24–26, NLT)

Later in the book of Joshua we see that Joseph's faith was rewarded:

'The bones of Joseph, which the Israelites had brought along with them
when they left Egypt, were buried at Shechem, in the plot of land Jacob
had bought from the sons of Hamor for 100 pieces of silver. This land
was located in the territory allotted to the descendants of Joseph.'
(Josh. 24:32, NLT)

So what was so remarkable about this final episode in Joseph's later life
that caused the writer of Hebrews to emphasise this particular act of
faith? In order to understand this more fully we need to look at both the
nature of Joseph's faith and then at what he was looking forward to.

What faith is

What was the 'faith' of Joseph and the great biblical heroes? The writer of
the Hebrews gives us a succinct definition:

'Now faith is the substance of things hoped for, the evidence of things
not seen.' (Heb. 11:1, NKJV)

From this we can see that faith is linked to hope but different to hope.
It is related to the unseen, yet is somehow very tangible, as implied
by the use of the two words 'substance' and 'evidence'. 'Substance'
(*hupostasis* in the Greek) has the sense of that which underlies a thing,
or the basis of something, and is often linked to the idea of holding
the 'title deeds' to something. 'Evidence' implies an inner confidence.
Joseph's faith was both sure and confident.

Moreover, Joseph's faith was true in another respect: it was both expressed
in words and in actions. Biblical faith is seen as a spoken faith. Whether it be

the faith Jesus exercised to curse the fig tree (Mark 11:20–22) or the faith we need to be saved (Rom. 10:8–10), true faith starts in the heart and flows out of the mouth. Joseph spoke out and declared his faith in the future. But faith not only needs to be spoken, it must be acted upon (see James 2:14–26). Most of the examples used in the great faith chapter of Hebrews 11 show the heroes demonstrating their faith through their actions, as in Abel offering the sacrifice, Noah building the ark and Abraham leaving his country and offering his son. Although Joseph obviously did not take his own bones to Canaan, he was sufficiently 'sure' of what God had promised that he acted upon what he believed, insisting that his brothers solemnly swear to take his bones out of Egypt. If we, too, want to grow in faith we must continually ensure that we not only believe with our hearts, but also speak out with mouths and step out in action, in line with what we believe God has spoken to us. I am not talking about acting presumptuously if God has not spoken, but rather speaking and acting boldly, knowing when He has.

If Joseph's faith was both in word and deed, it was also both personal and concerned with the broader purposes of God for His people. Joseph was clearly a man who was prepared to see the bigger picture. His faith was not just a 'selfish' faith that focused on getting God to meet his every whim, nor was it a 'quick fix' faith, which is sadly so often the case in the body of Christ today. Rather, it was a deep faith, which focused on God's long-term promises for His people. The contrast between the young 17-year-old dreamer and the mature leader is striking. No longer focused just on himself and his own elevation, he now seems to have fully grasped that his role in life was part of a much bigger plan that went before him and would carry on after him, based on a promise first made to his great-grandfather and fulfilled by his own descendants four centuries later. Such a perspective is particularly necessary for us today, especially those of us living in an essentially short-term, individualistic Western culture. Certainly, each of us has our own dream to dream and destiny to fulfil, but our own personal life goals must ultimately be viewed through the lens of the global, end-time purposes of an eternal God working through His Son, Jesus Christ.

That doesn't mean, however, that our faith cannot and should not be concerned with personal matters. It is important to note that Joseph's big picture perspective concerning the Exodus from Egypt and the return to Canaan also included a very definite confidence in his own personal participation in the fulfilment of God's promises, as represented by his very specific request concerning the future of his bones. God is a big God, but He cares intimately about every detail of our lives.

What faith looks forward to

So what exactly was Joseph looking forward to? At the most straightforward level he was simply prophesying the future deliverance of the people of Israel and their inheritance in the physical land of Canaan. Both of these events were, of course, pivotal for the future of the people of Israel and are of central importance in understanding the story of the Bible as a whole. But aside from this fundamental historical perspective, the Scriptures themselves make clear that there is both a typological and eschatological understanding of these events.

Typologically, Egypt is frequently depicted as the land of slavery, of being a place of bondage to the world, the flesh and the devil. The Exodus is likewise viewed as the greatest act of deliverance and salvation in the entire Old Testament and a foreshadowing of the even greater deliverance made available through Jesus, the true Passover Lamb. Significantly, also in Hebrews 11, Moses is described as having shunned the fleeting pleasures of sin (as represented by life in Egypt) for the greater treasure of knowing Christ. So, what was Joseph expressing in demonstrating his desire to be buried in Canaan? He was acknowledging at a deeper level that Egypt was not his true home, that the Egyptians were not his true people, and that the gods of Egypt were not his gods. Rather, he was stating that he belonged in the Promised Land, to the family of Jacob, and to the providential God of his fathers. As an heir to the Promised Land, he is a type of the believer who now has a wonderful inheritance in Christ.

But the clear implication of Hebrews 11 is that Joseph's insight into the Exodus and conquest of Canaan was not only typological but also eschatological (end-time). Abraham set the example, making his home in the Promised Land 'like a stranger in a foreign country' by living in tents: 'For he was looking forward to the city with foundations, whose architect and builder is God' (Heb. 11:9–10). He and the other patriarchs were, 'longing for a better country – a heavenly one. Therefore God is not ashamed to be called their God, for he has prepared a city for them' (Heb. 11:16). It seems reasonable to assume that in believing for the return to the land of Canaan, Joseph too was looking for a better country.

So, what is this heavenly country or city that these great heroes of faith were longing for? It is important to note that they were not looking so much for a heaven 'up there' but rather a 'heavenly country' or 'city' down here. This is an important corrective to much of what is taught today and a reminder that the focus of the Bible's teaching is eschatology not escapology! Certainly, there is clear evidence that when a Christian dies they go to be with Christ 'in heaven' or 'in paradise'. But this is a temporary or intermediate state when the spirit and soul of the person is kept in Christ prior to the Second Coming. But in the age to come, God comes down and we dwell in His city in the new earth. To quote from *The Message*:

'Look! Look! God has moved into the neighborhood, making his home with men and women! They're his people, he's their God. He'll wipe every tear from their eyes. Death is gone for good—tears gone, crying gone, pain gone—all the first order of things gone.' (Rev. 21:3–4)

And on that day, Joseph will be there. His once decayed bones will be resurrected with the rest of his body and united with his spirit and his soul. His dream will have been finally fulfilled.

A similar promise awaits us too. Like Joseph in Egypt, we must serve and work in this current culture without being conformed to it or making our 'home' in it. Rather, we must look forward to that great and final day, when Jesus will return and we, with Joseph and all God's people, will be reunited with Christ in our glorious new resurrection bodies in a wonderful new heaven on a new earth!

Epilogue

Joseph lived the dream, and so can you and I. Like him, we need first to dream God's dream for our lives. As we 'see' His vision and 'hear' His word for us, we can move forward with confidence, knowing that what He has sovereignly ordained and spoken will come to pass.

However, it is one thing to dream the dream; it is another to actually live it. Hence, we need to embrace God's unique preparation. This will undoubtedly involve passing tests that will help mature our character. Like Joseph, we will have to learn lessons, such as the importance of forgiving others, resisting sexual temptation, and prospering even when times seem tough.

Then we can get ready for promotion. This will require patience while we are waiting and also expectancy that God will open the right doors at the right time. When He does, we will need to be prepared for Him to work through the gifts He has already given us and to be faithful in the exercise of those gifts. Once we have been promoted we must make sure that we realise the purpose for our prosperity and that we are first and foremost blessed in order to be a blessing.

Throughout, we must be ready for relational reconciliation. If there are any unresolved issues of conflict with members of our families or God's family, in particular, we must be prepared, like Joseph, to wisely press through to a place of harmony and restoration. We must then, like him, determine that we are going to 'finish well' and serve God's purposes both within our families, our churches and the world, thereby leaving a great and eternal legacy for the generations to come.

Endnotes

[1]Charles Swindoll, *Great Lives Series: Joseph: A Man of Integrity and Forgiveness* (Nashville: WPublishing Group, 1998), p11.

[2]Many thanks to Rick Warren's *The Purpose Driven Life* (Grand Rapids: Zondervan, 2004) for the inspiration for these subheadings.

[3]Warren, *ibid.*, p213.

[4]Quote found at www.goodreads.com [accessed August 2016].

[5]Swindoll, *ibid.*, p76.

[6]Terry Virgo, *The Tide is Turning* (Weybridge: New Wine Press, 2006), p57.

[7]Walter Brueggemann, *Genesis: A Bible Commentary for Teaching and Preaching* (Louisville: John Knox Press, 1982), p340.

[8]For further reading, see Robert Candlish, *Studies in Genesis* (Grand Rapids: Kregel Publications, 1979).

[9]Liam Goligher, *Joseph: The Hidden Hand of God* (Scotland: Christian Focus, 2008), p114.

[10]Brueggemann, *ibid.*, p337.

[11]Goligher, *ibid.*, p109.

[12]Brueggemann, *ibid.*, p345.

[13]Brueggemann, *ibid.*, p347.

[14]Goligher, *ibid.*, p202.

[15]Claus Westermann, *Genesis 37–50: A Commentary* (Minneapolis: Augsburg Fortress, 1985), p310.

[16]Gordon J. Wenham, *Word Biblical Commentary 2: Genesis 16–50* (Grand Rapids: Zondervan, 1994), p447.

[17]Lindsay Wilson, *Joseph, Wise and Otherwise* (Eugene: Paternoster, 2006), p193.

[18]Brueggemann, *ibid.*, p356.

[19]Wenham, *ibid.*, p449.

[20]Bruce K. Waltke, *Genesis: A Commentary* (Grand Rapids: Zondervan, 2001), p589.

[21]Goligher, *ibid.*, p206.

[22]Brueggemann, *ibid.*, p365.

[23]Lloyd Reeb, *From Success to Significance* (Grand Rapids: Zondervan, 2004), pp14–15.

[24]Brueggemann, *ibid.*, p376.

Further reading

Baldwin, Joyce G., *The Message of Genesis 12–50* (Downers Grove: IVP, 1986).

Brueggemann, Walter, *Genesis: A Bible Commentary for Teaching and Preaching* (Louisville: John Knox Press, 1982).

Calvin, John, *Calvin's Bible Commentaries: Genesis* (London: Forgotten Books, 2007).

Candlish, Robert, *Studies in Genesis* (Grand Rapids: Kregel Publications, 1979).

Clinton, Robert J., *The Making of a Leader* (Colorado Springs: NavPress, 1988).

Cordeiro, Wayne, *The Divine Mentor* (Minnesota: Bethany House Publishers, 2007).

Goligher, Liam, *Joseph: The Hidden Hand of God* (Scotland: Christian Focus, 2008).

Hybels, Bill, *Holy Discontent* (Grand Rapids: Zondervan, 2007).

Kendall, R.T., *God Meant it for Good* (Eugene: Paternoster Press, 2003).

Morris, Robert, *From Dream to Destiny* (Minnesota: Bethany House Publishers, 2011).

Rad, Gerhard von, *Genesis: A Commentary* (Louisville: John Knox Press, 1972).

Reeb, Lloyd, *From Success to Significance* (Grand Rapids: Zondervan, 2004).

Storms, Sam, *Pleasures Evermore: The Life-Changing Power of Enjoying God* (Colorado Springs: NavPress, 2000).

Swindoll, Charles *Great Lives Series: Joseph: A Man of Integrity and Forgiveness* (Nashville: W Publishing Group, 1998).

Virgo, Terry, *The Tide is Turning* (Weybridge: New Wine Press, 2006).

Waltke, Bruce K., *Genesis: A Commentary* (Grand Rapids: Zondervan, 2001).

Warren, Rick, *The Purpose Driven Life* (Grand Rapids: Zondervan, 2004).

Wenham, Gordon J., *Word Biblical Commentary 2: Genesis 16–50* (Grand Rapids: Zondervan, 1994).

Westermann, Claus, *Genesis 37–50: A Commentary.* (Minneapolis: Augsburg Fortress, 1985).

Wilson, Lindsay, *Joseph, Wise and Otherwise* (Eugene: Paternoster Press, 2006).

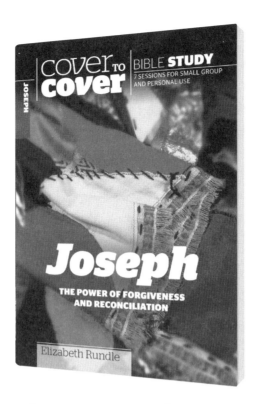

Delve deeper into the story of Joseph together

Explore the story of Joseph further with the *Cover to Cover* Bible study, *Joseph: The power of forgiveness and reconciliation*. Discover aspects of the geography, theology and humanity found in one of the Bible's most popular passages. Each of the seven sessions include an icebreaker, Bible readings, discussion starters and more. Ideal for individual and group use.

By Elizabeth Rundle

ISBN: 978-1-85345-252-9

RRP £3.99

For full range of *Cover to Cover* Bible studies and to order, go to **www.cwr.org.uk/store** call **01252 784700** or visit a Christian bookshop.

Church programmes
by Dave Smith

With FREE online resources

Using Ephesians 1–3, Transformed Life explores questions of our identity, purpose and belonging. This seven-week programme includes resources for the whole church, small groups and individuals. Underpinned by a 50-day devotional.

ISBN: 978-1-78259-412-3
RRP £6.99 (£4.99 for 10 or more copies)

www.transformed-life.info

Short Activity Book for Early Years
(for ages 3–6)
ISBN: 978-1-78259-442-0
RRP £3.50

Short Activity Book for Primary Years
(for ages 7–11)
ISBN: 978-1-78259-441-3
RRP £3.50

Building on the foundations laid in Transformed Life, this seven-week programme uses Ephesians 4–6 to explore how we can live out the Christian life. Ideal as a stand-alone programme, or as the second part of a series with Transformed Life. Underpinned by a 50-day devotional.

ISBN: 978-1-78259-587-8
RRP £6.99 (£4.99 for 10 or more copies)

www.transformed-living.info

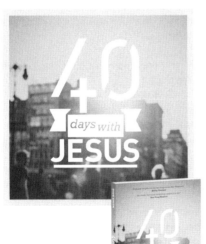

A post-Easter resource for individuals, small groups and churches. At the heart of this six-week programme is an invitation to actively explore the accounts of the risen Jesus. Underpinned by a 40-day devotional.

ISBN: 978-1-78259-138-2
RRP £6.99 (£4.99 for 10 or more copies)

www.40days.info

Courses and seminars

Waverley Abbey College

Publishing and media

Conference facilities

Transforming lives

CWR's vision is to enable people to experience personal transformation through applying God's Word to their lives and relationships.

Our Bible-based training and resources help people around the world to:
• Grow in their walk with God
• Understand and apply Scripture to their lives
• Resource themselves and their church
• Develop pastoral care and counselling skills
• Train for leadership
• Strengthen relationships, marriage and family life and much more.

Our insightful writers provide daily Bible reading notes and other resources for all ages, and our experienced course designers and presenters have gained an international reputation for excellence and effectiveness.

CWR's Training and Conference Centres in Surrey and East Sussex, England, provide excellent facilities in idyllic settings – ideal for both learning and spiritual refreshment.

CWR Applying God's Word to everyday life and relationships

CWR, Waverley Abbey House,
Waverley Lane, Farnham,
Surrey GU9 8EP, UK

Telephone: **+44 (0)1252 784700**
Email: info@cwr.org.uk
Website: www.cwr.org.uk

Registered Charity No. 294387
Company Registration No. 1990308